KNOWING

Random House
Studies in Philosophy

Consulting Editor:
V. C. CHAPPELL

KNOWING

Essays in the Analysis of Knowledge

Edited by

MICHAEL D. ROTH
Franklin and Marshall College

LEON GALIS
Franklin and Marshall College

Random House New York

Library of Congress Catalog Card Number: 75–114566

Manufactured in the United States of America. Printed and bound by Halliday Lithograph Corp., West Hanover, Mass.

98765432
First Edition

Preface

This book is a product of our frustration in trying to teach undergraduate seminars in epistemology. It appears to be a function of the philosophical naïveté of some undergraduates that no matter what special topic or sophisticated approach is offered them under the catalog description "Seminar in Epistemology," they will sooner or later ask, "But what exactly *is* knowledge? What does it *mean* to say that so and so knows that such and such?" After experiencing several such instances of undergraduate ingenuousness, we adopted the strategem of bringing the seminar down to a manageable level by restricting it to the question What is knowledge?

One immediate consequence of adopting such a strategem was that suitable texts had to be found. It was clear to us that in the last twenty-five years the best and most exciting literature on the question had been published subsequent to and largely in response to Edmund Gettier's important paper "Is Justified True Belief Knowledge?" which first appeared in 1963. Unfortunately most of these papers were scattered in various philosophical journals. The only feasible ways to make these papers available to students were to have them placed on the reserve shelf in the library or to have them reproduced. Neither of these alternatives proved satisfactory: in the former method, serious problems of accessibility were encountered; in the latter, equally serious problems of economics. It was at this time that we began thinking about collecting these articles in a single volume.

That said, some comments are now in order concerning the way in which the essays were selected and arranged. Only one of the two articles selected to appear under the heading "The Traditional Analysis of Knowledge" seems to belong there, and that is the excerpt from Ayer's *The Problem of Knowledge*. It is, in fact, this excerpt to which Gettier refers in "Is Justified True Belief Knowledge?" Malcolm's "Knowledge and Belief," on the other hand, appears at first to be conspicuously out of place. After all, Malcolm neither gives, nor attempts to give, anything like an analysis of knowledge, let alone a traditional analysis. Nevertheless, we felt that an arguable case could be made for saying that while Malcolm never argues explicitly for the view that knowledge is justified true belief, that view is a *consequence* of the views he does expound. Consider the following passage:

> As philosophers we may be surprised to observe that it *can* be that the knowledge that *p* is true should differ from the belief that *p* is true *only* in the respect that in one case *p* is true and in the other false. But that is the fact.

As Malcolm's examples make abundantly clear, the sort of case of false belief which, as he claims, differs from a case of knowledge in just this way is a case of *justified* false belief. But if the *only* difference between a case of justified false belief and a case of knowing is that in the former case *p* is false while in the latter case it is true, then knowing seems to be nothing other than justified true belief. It appears, then, that one of the consequences of accepting Malcolm's argument is the rejection of the validity of one or both of Gettier's counterexamples. Hence, the issue is joined.

We had also originally planned to include that part of Chisholm's *Perceiving* which is criticized by Gettier. However, Chisholm suggested using the present material entitled "The Foundation of Empirical Statements" not only because it more accurately represented his present views than did the passage from *Perceiving* but also because it originally appeared in a collection of essays published in Poland and not many English speaking philosophers had yet had the opportunity to read it. This, coupled with the fact that including the passage from *Perceiving* would not accomplish anything not already accomplished by including the Ayer selection, prompted us to decide in favor of the present selection. We wish to make grateful mention of the fact that Chisholm very kindly made extensive revisions in his paper in order to meet the needs of our book.

By far the most difficult task we had was deciding, from among the large number of unusually fine pieces on the Gettier paper, which to include and which to set aside. The existence of so many first-rate articles and the fact that this was to be a compact collection precluded not only the possibility of publishing every deserving paper but also the possibility of appealing only to the criterion of excellence in making our choices. We were forced to consider, as well, the availability of a selection in other anthologies, similarity of approach among selections, and even, alas, the length of a selection. It is, of course, a foregone conclusion that our selections will not be universally applauded, but that is, after all, the traditional lot of anthologies.

Finally, we have the pleasant task of acknowledging our debts. To Professor Keith Lehrer, whose encouragement, advice, and support were instrumental in bringing this book to publication, to Professors C. E. Caton and R. Swartz, whose many helpful suggestions and criticisms improved the book considerably, and to our student, Mr. Glenn Melton, who did yeoman service in helping us prepare the manuscript. Lastly, we are especially grateful to the individual contributors and their publishers for their kind permission to reprint the selections in this volume.

M. Roth
L. Galis

LANCASTER, PA.

Contents

KNOWING

Introduction

The following passage is taken from A. M. MacIver's Presidential Address to the Joint Session of the Aristotelian Society and the Mind Association. Although it was written slightly more than ten years ago, the editors believe that it is an appropriate introductory statement to the present collection of essays.

There have been philosophers, from the Platonic (and probably also the historical) Socrates onward, who have conceived the business of philosophy to be to make clear the meanings of ordinary words. Their paradigm of philosophy is the typical Platonic dialogue. It is asked, for example, "What is temperance?" and the answer is found by taking the interlocutor as a standard user of language and making him consider when he would, and when he would not, call a man or an action "temperate." But this does not represent an interest in words for their own sake. It is assumed that to each word there corresponds something for which it stands, so that consideration of the way in which the word is used reveals the nature of what it stands for.

This procedure would only be reliable if it could be taken for granted that every word of ordinary language always meant the same thing. It was very soon discovered that this is not the case. Wittgenstein's dictum that "all the propositions of ordinary speech are already logically quite in order" is only true in the sense that ordinary language, competently used, can always do whatever it is designed to do. The parts played by all the words used in any particular utterance can always be made clear in the circumstances of the utterance. It does not follow that the words must play the same parts when used in other utterances. That is why philosophy needs technical terms—or else those complicated circumlocutions, that complex talk about "logical grammar" and the like, which is the substitute for technical terms adopted by those who deny themselves the use of them.

I allow that there is truth behind the belief that philosophers have to explain ordinary words. Professor Ayer, I think, went too far—or at least used language which could easily be misinterpreted—when he wrote: "Philosophers, like scientists, are at liberty to introduce technical terms, or to use ordinary words in a technical sense."[1] Philosophers are indeed free, as scientists are free, to coin technical terms, but they have not the same freedom. The philosopher is tied to the uses of ordinary language in a way in which the scientist is not, because it is only by reference to ordinary linguistic usage that he can explain what his technical terms are designed to mean. A botanist can explain what he means by "bract" or "sepal" by pointing to a typical plant, or several plants, or by drawing a diagram. A chemist can introduce the term "valency" by listing a number of facts experimentally established and showing that a certain use of the term "valency" enables these facts to be compendiously stated. The philosopher cannot in the same way point to anything outside the use of language itself. He can only explain that he means by a technical term what would be meant by some ordinary word or words used in some particular circumstances.

But here the words "in some particular circumstances" are vital. When a philosopher tackles (say) the Theory of Perception, he has to start from ways in which everyone uses such words as "see" and "hear." But this does not mean that he simply asks how these words are used and stops there. You are much more likely to find him asking whether there is a difference, and, if so, what, between what anyone would mean by "see" when he said that a keen-sighted man "can see a star of the sixth magnitude with the naked eye" and when he said that a man who has slipped and cracked his head on the cellar floor "sees stars." It is at this point that he is likely to introduce philosophical technical terms, such as "percept" and "sense-

[1] *The Problem of Knowledge* (Pelican Books, 1956), p. 18.

datum." Though they have to be introduced by a reference to ordinary linguistic usages, they are not said to be simply equivalent to any ordinary expressions—if they were only *that,* then there would be no need to introduce them, for the ordinary expressions would do as well—but to be equivalent to ordinary expressions only as used in specified kinds of contexts. Every language economises in words, as a small theatrical company economises in actors, making one word play many parts, which normally causes no difficulty in communication, because context makes most things clear. But a philosopher needs to distinguish a word playing one part from the same word playing another part, and for that it is convenient to have a technical terminology in which the parts are played by different words.

This evening I want to apply these general reflections to the special case of the family of words, "know," "knowledge," and their kindred. Though one would have expected modern philosophers to be too sophisticated for this, it seems to me that even in contemporary discussions of "knowing" a Socratic or Platonic simple-mindedness still prevails.

Here we have an actual Platonic dialogue to start from—the *Theaetetus.* Its formula is the standard one. The question being "What is knowledge?" Theaetetus suggests various answers, each of which in turn Socrates forces him to abandon by making him admit that there are cases in which the suggested conditions would be satisfied to which the word "know" would not be applied. I seem to hear echoes of the *Theaetetus* in modern discussions of the same subject from Cook Wilson to Ayer, but particularly in Chapter XIII of Russell's *Problems of Philosophy* (where I suspect that many of my generation encountered the subject for the first time). The general line of argument can be indicated by drawing examples from Plato and Russell indiscriminately.

One suggested answer to the question is that "knowledge" means simply *true belief,* but to this it is objected that there are cases of true belief which would not be called "knowledge." Plato takes an example from the Athenian law-courts, where juries were notoriously swayed more by the oratorical skill of the parties than by any evidence brought forward, but it would be absurd to think that they *always* found the innocent guilty and the guilty innocent. There being only two possibilities, pure chance would make them believe the tale told by the right side roughly every other time, and then they would *believe truly,* but, as they would not believe with any rational grounds, they would not be said to "know." Can it be said, then, that knowledge is true belief *rationally grounded?* Not if all that is meant by this is that it is validly deduced from premisses, because the premisses might be false. Russell, writing in 1912, under the Asquith government, uses the example of a man who had forgotten the short-lived Bannerman administration and thought that the last Prime Minister had been Balfour. He would believe truly that the last Prime Minister's name began with B, and believe this for a reason, but he would not be said to "know" that the last Prime Minister's name began with B, because he inferred this from a belief which was false. Suppose then we say that knowledge is true belief based on valid inference from premisses which themselves are true. This (with a little obviously necessary sophistication to cover the case of so-called "intuitive knowledge") is the pont at which those who argue on these lines nowadays usually seem content to stop. But the question still arises, why these true premisses are believed. If I believe P without reason, but it happens that P is true, it seems odd that I should *not* be said to "know" P, but *should* be said to "know" Q, which I believe only because I infer it from P. As the Platonic Socrates puts it on the last page of the *Theaetetus,* to make belief count as "knowledge" we want to say that it must not only be true, and inferred from premisses which are true, but inferred from premisses which are *known,* but this makes the definition of knowledge circular.

The conclusion which Plato himself drew from this was that knowledge could not be defined as any species of belief, but must be reckoned something generically different. The same conclusion has been drawn in modern times by Cook Wilson and the Cook Wilsonians, notably Prichard. But, if knowledge and belief are quite different in kind, it is oddly difficult ever to tell which is which. Whatever knowledge may be, it is agreed that it is impossible to know what is not the case. But people sometimes claim to know what even they themselves later allow not to have been the case. It follows that they did not know, but only believed, what they falsely believed themselves to know. But what is the difference between believing that one knows when one does not know and merely believing? If the distinction of knowledge from belief is to have any value, I must be able, at least sometimes, not only to know but to know that I know. But then do I know that I know that I know, or only believe (whether truly or falsely) that I know that I know, and so still only believe (perhaps falsely) that I know, and so perhaps still only believe falsely?

The discussion here is not simply about the way in which the word "know" is actually used. Even Prichard, I think, would have allowed that there might be a loose usage in which "know" meant just "believe truly," though he would have said that this was *incorrect*—a way in which uneducated journalists might perhaps use the word, but not responsible speakers of good English like Prichard himself. The discussion starts rather from the other end. It is assumed that there is something, for which we need to have a name, for which "know" is the name that our language in fact provides. But we want to discover exactly what that something is. This we can do (it is alleged or assumed) by considering how we use the word "know" when we speak carefully.*

Implicit in the last few paragraphs of MacIver's statement is the suggestion that a proper analysis of knowledge is one that proceeds almost organically. To raise the Socratic question What is knowledge? is, for contemporary philosophers, equivalent to asking whether the traditional analysis of knowledge as justified true belief is correct. But any attempt to provide a thorough assessment of the traditional analysis must ultimately consider the objection, which is at least as old as Plato's *Republic*, that knowledge is not a kind of belief at all. According to this objection, knowing something to be true and believing something to be true are *entirely* separate and distinct and neither can legitimately occur in the analysis of the other. In recent years the most common way of raising this objection has been to ask whether knowing *entails* believing. To see how this way of putting the question simplifies the issue without in any way avoiding it, one need only try to maintain consistently either that knowledge entails belief but

* A. M. MacIver, "Knowledge," *Proceedings of the Aristotelian Society,* Supp. Vol. 32 (1958), 1–5. Reprinted by courtesy of the Editor of The Aristotelian Society. Copyright 1958 by The Aristotelian Society.

cannot be analyzed in terms of it or that knowledge is analyzable in terms of belief but does not entail it.

The question of the relation of knowledge to belief produces further complexities in the analysis of knowledge. As MacIver suggests, people who claim to know and then turn out to be mistaken are sometimes said to have believed that they knew. But why should one only be said to believe that he knows when he happens to be wrong? It would seem that if one can believe knowledge claims which turn out to be false, then he is surely entitled to believe those which turn out to be true. It is prima facie absurd to suppose that a difference between false knowledge claims and true ones is that we believe the former but not the latter.

Moreover, if we can be said to believe our knowledge claims, regardless of their truth value, why shouldn't we be able to doubt them as well. Again, it appears to be a mere truism (despite Descartes!) that whatever is capable of being believed is capable of being doubted. There are no necessary truths of the form 'X believes that p'. But this suggests that one can know something to be true and, at the same time, doubt that he knows it. If this view is correct then either knowing does not entail believing or it is possible for someone to know something and not know that he knows it. If knowing entails believing and if it is possible to know without believing that one knows, then knowing is not the same as knowing that one knows.

Thus the question of whether knowing entails knowing that one knows can be seen to depend, in part at least, on the question of whether knowing entails believing. And, as we have already seen, this question itself depends in part on the question of whether the traditional analysis of knowledge is correct. The arrangement of the selections that follow is intended to reflect, as clearly as possible, the interrelation of the issues we have tried to present briefly here.

PART ONE

THE TRADITIONAL ANALYSIS OF KNOWLEDGE

A. J. Ayer

Knowing As Having the Right To Be Sure

The answers which we have found for the questions we have so far been discussing have not yet put us in a position to give a complete account of what it is to know that something is the case. The first requirement is that what is known should be true, but this is not sufficient; not even if we add to it the further condition that one must be completely sure of what one knows. For it is possible to be completely sure of something which is in fact true, but yet not to know it. The circumstances may be such that one is not entitled to be sure. For instance, a superstitious person who had inadvertently walked under a ladder might be convinced as a result that he was about to suffer some misfortune; and he might in fact be right. But it would not be correct to say that he knew that this was going to be so. He arrived at his belief by a process of reasoning which would not be generally reliable; so, although his prediction came true, it was not a case of knowledge. Again, if someone were fully persuaded of a mathematical proposition by a proof which could be shown to be invalid, he would not, without further evidence, be said to know the proposition, even though it was true. But while it is not hard to find examples of true and fully confident beliefs which in some

From *The Problem of Knowledge* by A. J. Ayer (Penguin Books, 1956), pp. 31–35. Reprinted by permission of Penguin Books.

11

ways fail to meet the standards required for knowledge, it is
not at all easy to determine exactly what these standards are.

One way of trying to discover them would be to consider
what would count as satisfactory answers to the question
How do you know? Thus people may be credited with knowing truths of mathematics or logic if they are able to give a
valid proof of them, or even if, without themselves being able
to set out such a proof, they have obtained this information
from someone who can. Claims to know empirical statements
may be upheld by a reference to perception, or to memory,
or to testimony, or to historical records, or to scientific laws.
But such backing is not always strong enough for knowledge.
Whether it is so or not depends upon the circumstances of the
particular case. If I were asked how I knew that a physical
object of a certain sort was in such and such a place, it would,
in general, be a sufficient answer for me to say that I could see
it; but if my eyesight were bad and the light were dim, this
answer might not be sufficient. Even though I was right, it
might still be said that I did not really know that the object
was there. If I have a poor memory and the event which I
claim to remember is remote, my memory of it may still not
amount to knowledge, even though in this instance it does not
fail me. If a witness is unreliable, his unsupported evidence
may not enable us to know that what he says is true, even in
a case where we completely trust him and he is not in fact
deceiving us. In a given instance it is possible to decide
whether the backing is strong enough to justify a claim to
knowledge. But to say in general how strong it has to be would
require our drawing up a list of the conditions under which
perception, or memory, or testimony, or other forms of evidence are reliable. And this would be a very complicated
matter, if indeed it could be done at all.

Moreover, we cannot assume that, even in particular instances, an answer to the question How do you know? will
always be forthcoming. There may very well be cases in
which one knows that something is so without its being possible to say how one knows it. I am not so much thinking now
of claims to know facts of immediate experience, statements

like 'I know that I feel pain', which raise problems of their own into which we shall enter later on. In cases of this sort it may be argued that the question how one knows does not arise. But even when it clearly does arise, it may not find an answer. Suppose that someone were consistently successful in predicting events of a certain kind, events, let us say, which are not ordinarily thought to be predictable, like the results of a lottery. If his run of successes were sufficiently impressive, we might very well come to say that he knew which number would win, even though he did not reach this conclusion by any rational method, or indeed by any method at all. We might say that he knew it by intuition, but this would be to assert no more than that he did know it but that we could not say how. In the same way, if someone were consistently successful in reading the minds of others without having any of the usual sort of evidence, we might say that he knew these things telepathically. But in default of any further explanation this would come down to saying merely that he did know them, but not by an ordinary means. Words like 'intuition' and 'telepathy' are brought in just to disguise the fact that no explanation has been found.

But if we allow this sort of knowledge to be even theoretically possible, what becomes of the distinction between knowledge and true belief? How does our man who knows what the results of the lottery will be differ from one who only makes a series of lucky guesses? The answer is that, so far as the man himself is concerned, there need not be any difference. His procedure and his state of mind, when he is said to know what will happen, may be exactly the same as when it is said that he is only guessing. The difference is that to say that he knows is to concede to him the right to be sure, while to say that he is only guessing is to withhold it. Whether we make this concession will depend upon the view which we take of his performance. Normally we do not say that people know things unless they have followed one of the accredited routes to knowledge. If someone reaches a true conclusion without appearing to have any adequate basis for it, we are likely to say that he does not really know it. But if he were repeatedly

successful in a given domain, we might very well come to say
that he knew the facts in question, even though we could not
explain how he knew them. We should grant him the right
to be sure, simply on the basis of his success. This is, indeed,
a point on which people's views might be expected to differ.
Not everyone would regard a successful run of predictions,
however long sustained, as being by itself a sufficient backing
for a claim to knowledge. And here there can be no question
of proving that this attitude is mistaken. Where there are
recognized criteria for deciding when one has the right to be
sure, anyone who insists that their being satisfied is still not
enough for knowledge may be accused, for what the charge
is worth, of misusing the verb 'to know'. But it is possible
to find, or at any rate to devise, examples which are not
covered in this respect by any established rule of usage.
Whether they are to count as instances of knowledge is then
a question which we are left free to decide.

It does not, however, matter very greatly which decision
we take. The main problem is to state and assess the grounds
on which these claims to knowledge are made, to settle, as
it were, the candidate's marks. It is a relatively unimportant
question what titles we then bestow upon them. So long as
we agree about the marking, it is of no great consequence
where we draw the line between pass and failure, or between
the different levels of distinction. If we choose to set a very
high standard, we may find ourselves committed to saying
that some of what ordinarily passes for knowledge ought
rather to be described as probable opinion. And some critics
will then take us to task for flouting ordinary usage. But the
question is purely one of terminology. It is to be decided, if
at all, on grounds of practical convenience.

One must not confuse this case, where the markings are
agreed upon, and what is in dispute is only the bestowal of
honours, with the case where it is the markings themselves
that are put in question. For this second case is philosophically important, in a way in which the other is not. The
sceptic who asserts that we do not know all that we think we
know, or even perhaps that we do not strictly know anything

at all, is not suggesting that we are mistaken when we conclude that the recognized criteria for knowing have been
satisfied. Nor is he primarily concerned with getting us to
revise our usage of the verb 'to know', any more than one
who challenges our standards of value is trying to make us
revise our usage of the word 'good'. The disagreement is
about the application of the word, rather than its meaning.
What the sceptic contends is that our markings are too high;
that the grounds on which we are normally ready to concede
the right to be sure are worth less than we think; he may even
go so far as to say that they are not worth anything at all. The
attack is directed, not against the way in which we apply our
standards of proof, but against these standards themselves.
It has, as we shall see, to be taken seriously because of the
arguments by which it is supported.

I conclude then that the necessary and sufficient conditions
for knowing that something is the case are first that what one
is said to know be true, secondly that one be sure of it, and
thirdly that one should have the right to be sure. This right
may be earned in various ways; but even if one could give a
complete description of them it would be a mistake to try to
build it into the definition of knowledge, just as it would be a
mistake to try to incorporate our actual standards of goodness
into a definition of good. And this being so, it turns out that
the questions which philosophers raise about the possibility
of knowledge are not all to be settled by discovering what
knowledge is. For many of them reappear as questions about
the legitimacy of the title to be sure. They need to be severally
examined; and this is the main concern of what is called the
theory of knowledge.

Norman Malcolm

Knowledge and Belief

"We must recognize that when we know something we either do, or by reflecting, can know that our condition is one of knowing that thing, while when we believe something, we either do or can know that our condition is one of believing and not of knowing: so that we cannot mistake belief for knowledge or vice versa."[1]

This remark is worthy of investigation. Can I discover *in myself* whether I know something or merely believe it?

Let us begin by studying the ordinary usage of "know" and "believe." Suppose, for example, that several of us intend to go for a walk and that you propose that we walk in Cascadilla Gorge. I protest that I should like to walk beside a flowing stream and that at this season the gorge is probably dry. Consider the following cases:

(1) You say "I believe that it won't be dry although I have no particular reason for thinking so." If we went to the gorge and found a flowing stream we should not say that you *knew* that there would be water but that you thought so and were right.

From *Knowledge and Certainty: Essays and Lectures* by Norman Malcolm (Prentice-Hall, 1963), pp. 58–72. Reprinted by permission of Prentice-Hall, Inc.

[1] H. A. Prichard, *Knowledge and Perception* (Oxford: The Clarendon Press, 1950), p. 88.

(2) You say "I believe that it won't be dry because it rained only three days ago and usually water flows in the gorge for at least that long after a rain." If we found water we should be inclined to say that you knew that there would be water. It would be quite natural for you to say "I knew that it wouldn't be dry"; and we should tolerate your remark. This case differs from the previous one in that here you had a *reason*.

(3) You say "I know that it won't be dry" and give the same reason as in (2). If we found water we should have very little hesitation in saying that you knew. Not only had you a reason, but you *said* "I know" instead of "I believe." It may seem to us that the latter should not make a difference—but it does.

(4) You say "I know that it won't be dry" and give a stronger reason, e.g., "I saw a lot of water flowing in the gorge when I passed it this morning." If we went and found water, there would be no hesitation at all in saying that you knew. If, for example, we later met someone who said "Weren't you surprised to see water in the gorge this afternoon?" you would reply "No, I *knew* that there would be water; I had been there earlier in the day." We should have no objection to this statement.

(5) Everything happens as in (4), except that upon going to the gorge we find it to be dry. We should not say that you knew, but that you *believed* that there would be water. And this is true even though you declared that you knew, and even though your evidence was the same as it was in case (4) in which you did know.

I wish to make some comments on the usage of "know," "knew," "believe," and "believed," as illustrated in the preceding cases:

(a) Whether we should say that you knew, depends in part on whether you had grounds for your assertion and on the strength of those grounds. There would certainly be less hesitation to say that you knew in case (4) than in case (3), and this can be due only to the difference in the strength of the grounds.

(b) Whether we should say that you knew, depends in part on how *confident* you were. In case (2), if you had said "It rained only three days ago and usually water flows in the gorge for at least that long after a rain; but, of course, I don't feel absolutely sure that there will be water," then we should *not* have said that you knew that there would be water. If you lack confidence that p is true, then others do not say that you know that p is true, even though *they* know that p is true. Being confident is a necessary condition for knowing.

(*c*) Prichard says that if we reflect we cannot mistake belief for knowledge. In case (4) you knew that there would be water, and in case (5) you merely believed it. Was there any way that you could have discovered by reflection, in case (5), that you did not know? It would have been useless to have reconsidered your grounds for saying that there would be water, because in case (4), where you *did* know, your grounds were identical. They could be at fault in (5) only if they were at fault in (4), and they were not at fault in (4). Cases (4) and (5) differ in only one respect—namely, that in one case you did subsequently find water and in the other you did not. Prichard says that we can determine by reflection whether we know something or merely believe it. But where, in these cases, is the material that reflection would strike upon? There is none.

There is only one way that Prichard could defend his position. He would have to say that in case (4) you did *not* know that there would be water. And it is obvious that he would have said this. But this is false. It is an enormously common usage of language to say, in commenting upon just such an incident as (4), "He knew that the gorge wouldn't be dry because he had seen water flowing there that morning." It is a usage that all of us are familiar with. We so employ "know" and "knew" every day of our lives. We do not think of our usage as being loose or incorrect—and it is not. As philosophers we may be surprised to observe that it *can* be that the knowledge that p is true should differ from the belief that p is true *only* in the respect that in one case p is true and in the other false. But that is the fact.

There is an argument that one is inclined to use as a proof that you did not know that there would be water. The argument is the following: It could have turned out that you found no water; if it had so turned out you would have been mistaken in saying that you would find water; therefore you could have been mistaken; but if you could have been mistaken then you did not know.

Now it certainly *could* have turned out that the gorge was quite dry when you went there, even though you saw lots of water flowing through it only a few hours before. This does not show, however, that you did not know that there would be water. What it shows is that *although you knew you could have been mistaken.*[2] This would seem to be a contradictory result; but it is not. It seems so because our minds are fixed upon another usage of "know" and "knew"; one in which "It could have turned out that I was mistaken," implies "I did not know."

When is "know" used in this sense? I believe that Prichard uses it in this sense when he says that when we go through the proof of the proposition that the angles of a triangle are equal to two right angles we *know* that the proposition is true (p. 89). He says that if we put to ourselves the question: Is our condition one of knowing this, or is it only one of being convinced of it? then "We can only answer 'Whatever may be our state on other occasions, here we are knowing this.' And this statement is an expression of our *knowing* that we are knowing; for we do not *believe* that we are knowing this, we know that we are" (p. 89). He goes on to say that if someone were to object that we might be making a mistake "because for all we know we can later on discover some fact which is incompatible with a triangle's having angles that are equal to two right angles, we can answer that we *know* that there can be no such fact, for in knowing that a triangle must have such

---

[2] Some readers seem to have thought that I was denying here that "I knew that *p*" entails "that *p*." That was not my intention, and my words do not have that implication. If I had said *"although you knew you were mistaken,"* I should have denied the above entailment and, also, I should have misused "knew." The difference between the strong and weak senses of "know" (and "knew") is not that this entailment holds for the strong but not for the weak sense. It holds for both. If it is false that *p*, then one does not (and did not) know that *p*.

angles we also know that nothing can exist which is incompatible with this fact" (p. 90).

It is easy to imagine a non-philosophical context in which it would have been natural for Prichard to have said "I know that the angles of a triangle are equal to two right angles." Suppose that a young man just begining the study of geometry was in doubt as to whether that proposition is true, and had even constructed an ingenious argument that appeared to prove it false. Suppose that Prichard was unable to find any error in the argument. He might have said to the young man: "There must be an error in it. I know that the angles of a triangle are equal to two right angles."

When Prichard says that "nothing can exist which is incompatible with" the truth of that proposition, is he prophesying that no one will ever have the ingenuity to construct a flawless-looking argument against it? I believe not. When Prichard says that "we" *know* (and implies that *he* knows) that the proposition is true and *know* that nothing can exist that is incompatible with its being true, he is not making any *prediction* as to what the future will bring in the way of arguments or measurements. On the contrary, he is asserting that *nothing* that the future might bring could ever count as evidence against the proposition. He is implying that he would not *call* anything "evidence" against it. He is using "know" in what I shall call its "strong" sense. "Know" is used in this sense when a person's statement "I know that *p* is true" implies that the person who makes the statement would look upon nothing whatever as evidence that *p* is false.

It must not be assumed that whenever "know" is used in connection with mathematical propositions it is used in the strong sense. A great many people have *heard* of various theorems of geometry, e.g., the Pythagorean. These theorems are a part of "common knowledge." If a schoolboy doing his geometry assignment felt a doubt about the Pythagorean theorem, and said to an adult "Are you *sure* that it is true?" the latter might reply "Yes, I know that it is." He might make this reply even though he could not give proof of it and even though he had never gone through a proof of it. If subse-

quently he was presented with a "demonstration" that the
theorem is false, or if various persons reputed to have a knowledge of geometry soberly assured him that it is false, he might
be filled with doubt or even be convinced that he was mistaken. When he said "Yes, I know that it is true," he did not
pledge himself to hold to the theorem through thick and thin.
He did not absolutely exclude the possibility that something
could prove it to be false. I shall say that he used "know" in
the "weak" sense.

Consider another example from mathematics of the difference between the strong and weak senses of "know." I have
just now rapidly calculated that 92 times 16 is 1472. If I had
done this in the commerce of daily life where a practical problem was at stake, and if someone had asked "Are you sure that
$92 \times 16 = 1472$?" I might have answered "I *know* that it is; I
have just now calculated it." But also I might have answered
"I know that it is; but I will calculate it again to *make sure*."
And here my language points to a distinction. I say that I
know that $92 \times 16 = 1472$. Yet I am willing to *confirm* it—
that is, there is something that I should *call* "making sure";
and, likewise, there is something that I should *call* "finding
out that it is false." If I were to do this calculation again and
obtain the result that $92 \times 16 = 1372$, and if I were to carefully check this latter calculation without finding any error, I
should be disposed to say that I was previously mistaken when
I declared that $92 \times 16 = 1472$. Thus when I say that I know
that $92 \times 16 = 1472$, I allow for the possibility of a *refutation;*
and so I am using "know" in its weak sense.

Now consider propositions like $2 + 2 = 4$ and $7 + 5 = 12$. It
is hard to think of circumstances in which it would be natural
for me to say that I know that $2 + 2 = 4$, because no one ever
questions it. Let us try to suppose, however, that someone
whose intelligence I respect argues that certain developments
in arithmetic have shown that $2 + 2$ does not equal 4. He
writes out a proof of this in which I can find no flaw. Suppose
that his demeanor showed me that he was in earnest. Suppose
that several persons of normal intelligence became persuaded
that his proof was correct and that $2 + 2$ does not equal 4.

What would be my reaction? I should say "I can't see what is wrong with your proof; but it *is* wrong, because I *know* that $2 + 2 = 4$." Here I should be using "know" in its strong sense. I should not admit that any argument or any future development in mathematics could show that it is false that $2 + 2 = 4$.

The propositions $2 + 2 = 4$ and $92 \times 16 = 1472$ do not have the same status. There *can* be a demonstration that $2 + 2 = 4$. But a demonstration would be for me (and for any average person) only a curious exercise, a sort of *game*. We have no serious interest in proving that proposition.[3] It does not *need* a proof. It stands without one, and would not fall if a proof went against it. The case is different with the proposition that $92 \times 16 = 1472$. We take an interest in the demonstration (calculation) because the proposition *depends* upon its demonstration. A calculation may lead me to reject it as false. But $2 + 2 = 4$ does *not* depend on its demonstration. It does not depend on anything! And in the calculation that proves that $92 \times 16 = 1472$, there are steps that do not depend on any calculation (e.g., $2 \times 6 = 12$; $5 + 2 = 7$; $5 + 9 = 14$).

There is a correspondence between this dualism in the logical status of mathematical propositions and the two senses of "know." When I use "know" in the weak sense I am prepared to let an investigation (demonstration, calculation) determine whether the something that I claim to know is true or false. When I use "know" in the strong sense I am not prepared to look upon anything as an *investigation;* I do not concede that anything whatsoever could prove me mistaken; I do not regard the matter as open to any *question;* I do not admit that my proposition could turn out to be false, that any future investigation *could* refute it or cast doubt on it.[4]

---

[3] Some logicians and philosophers have taken an interest in proving that $2 + 2 = 4$ (e.g., Leibniz, *New Essays on the Understanding*, Bk. IV, ch. 7, sec. 10; Frege, *The Foundations of Arithmetic*, sec. 6). They have wished to show that it can be deduced from certain premises, and to determine what premises and rules of inference are required in the deduction. Their interest has not been in the *outcome* of the deduction.

[4] Compare these remarks about the strong sense of "know" with some of Locke's statements about "intuitive knowledge": ". . . in this the

We have been considering the strong sense of "know" in its application to mathematical propositions. Does it have application anywhere in the realm of *empirical* propositions—for example, to propositions that assert or imply that certain physical things exist? Descartes said that we have a "moral assurance" of the truth of some of the latter propositions but that we lack a "metaphysical certainty."[5] Locke said that the perception of the existence of physical things is not "so certain as our intuitive knowledge, or the deductions of our reason" although "it is an assurance that deserves the name of knowledge."[6] Some philosophers have held that when we make judgments of perception such as that there are peonies in the garden, cows in the field, or dishes in the cupboard, we are "taking for granted" that the peonies, cows, and dishes exist, but not knowing it in the "strict" sense. Others have held that all empirical propositions, including judgments of perception, are merely hypotheses.[7] The thought behind this exaggerated mode of expression is that any empirical proposition whatever *could* be refuted by future experience—that is, it *could* turn out to be false. Are these philosophers right?

Consider the following propositions:

(i) The sun is about ninety million miles from the earth.
(ii) There is a heart in my body.
(iii) Here is an ink-bottle.

In various circumstances I should be willing to assert of each of these propositions that I know it to be true. Yet they differ

---

mind is at no pains of proving or examining. . . ." "This part of knowledge . . . leaves no room for hesitation, doubt, or examination. . . ."

"It is on this intuition that depends all the certainty and evidence of all our knowledge; which certainly every one finds to be so great, that he cannot imagine, and therefore not require a greater. . . ." Locke, *Essay*, Bk. IV, ch. 2, sec. 1.

[5] Descartes, *Discourse on the Method*, Part IV.

[6] Locke, *Essay*, Book IV, ch. 11, sec. 3.

[7] E.g., ". . . no proposition, other than a tautology, can possibly be anything more than a probable hypothesis." A. J. Ayer, *Language, Truth and Logic*, second ed. (New York: Dover Publications, Inc., 1951), p. 38.

strikingly. This I see when, with each, I try to imagine the possibility that it is false.

(i) If in ordinary conversation someone said to me "The sun is about twenty million miles from the earth, isn't it?" I should reply "No, it is about ninety million miles from us." If he said "I think that you are confusing the sun with Polaris," I should reply "I *know* that ninety million miles is roughly the sun's distance from the earth." I might invite him to verify the figure in an encyclopedia. A third person who overheard our conversation could quite correctly report that I knew the distance to the sun, whereas the other man did not. But this knowledge of mine is little better than hearsay. I have seen that figure mentioned in a few books. I know nothing about the observations and calculations that led astronomers to accept it. If tomorrow a group of eminent astronomers announced that a great error had been made and that the correct figure is twenty million miles, I should not insist that they were wrong. It would surprise me that such an enormous mistake could have been made. But I should no longer be willing to say that I *know* that ninety million is the correct figure. Although I should *now* claim that I know the distance to be about ninety million miles, it is easy for me to envisage the possibility that some future investigation will prove this to be false.

(ii) Suppose that after a routine medical examination the excited doctor reports to me that the X-ray photographs show that I have no heart. I should tell him to get a new machine. I should be inclined to say that the fact that I have a heart is one of the few things that I can count on as absolutely certain. I can feel it beat. I know it's there. Furthermore, how could my blood circulate if I didn't have one? Suppose that later on I suffer a chest injury and undergo a surgical operation. Afterwards the astonished surgeons solemnly declare that they searched my chest cavity and found no heart, and that they made incisions and looked about in other likely places but found it not. They are convinced that I am without a heart. They are unable to understand how circulation can occur or what accounts for the thumping in my chest. But they are in agreement and obviously sincere, and they have clear photographs of my interior spaces. What would be my attitude? Would it be to insist that they were all mistaken? I think not. I believe that I should eventually accept their testimony and the evidence of the photographs. I should consider to be false what I now regard as an absolute certainty.

(iii) Suppose that as I write this paper someone in the next room were to call out to me "I can't find an ink-bottle; is there one in the house?" I should reply "Here is an ink-bottle." If he said in a doubtful tone "Are you sure? I looked there before," I should reply "Yes, I know there is; come and get it."

Now could it turn out to be false that there is an ink-bottle directly in front of me on this desk? Many philosophers have thought so. They would say that many things could happen of such a nature that if they did happen it would be proved that I am deceived. I agree that many extraordinary things could happen, in the sense that there is no logical absurdity in the supposition. It could happen that when I next reach for this ink-bottle my hand should seem to pass *through* it and I should not feel the contact of any object. It could happen that in the next moment the ink-bottle will suddenly vanish from sight; or that I should find myself under a tree in the garden with no ink-bottle about; or that one or more persons should enter this room and declare with apparent sincerity that they see no ink-bottle on this desk; or that a photograph taken now of the top of the desk should clearly show all of the objects on it except the ink-bottle. Having admitted that these things *could happen*,[8] am I compelled to admit that if they

---

[8] My viewpoint is somewhat different here from what it is in "The Verification Argument." There I am concerned with bringing out the different ways in which such a remark as "these things *could* happen" can be taken. I wish to show, furthermore, that from none of the senses in which the remark is *true* does it follow that it is *not certain* that the things in question will *not* happen. Finally, I hold there, that it is perfectly certain that they will not happen. Here, I am not disagreeing with any of those points, but I am adding the further point that my admission that, in some sense, the things *could happen,* does not require me to admit that *if* they were to happen, that would be evidence that there is no ink-bottle here now.

did happen then it would be proved that there is no ink-bottle here *now?* Not at all! I could say that when my hand seemed to pass through the ink-bottle I should *then* be suffering from hallucination; that if the ink-bottle suddenly vanished it would have miraculously ceased to exist; that the other persons were conspiring to drive me mad, or were themselves victims of remarkable concurrent hallucinations; that the camera possessed some strange flaw or that there was trickery in developing the negative. I admit that in the next moment I could find myself under a tree or in the bathtub. But this is not to admit that it could be revealed in the next moment that I am now dreaming. For what I admit is that I might be instantaneously transported to the garden, but not that in the next moment I might *wake up* in the garden. There is nothing that could happen to me in the next moment that I should call "waking up"; and therefore nothing that could happen to me in the next moment would be accepted by me now as proof that I now dream.

Not only do I not *have* to admit that those extraordinary occurrences would be evidence that there is no ink-bottle here; the fact is that I *do not* admit it. There is nothing whatever that could happen in the next moment or the next year that would by me be called *evidence* that there is not an ink-bottle here now. No future experience or investigation could prove to me that I am mistaken. Therefore, if I were to say "I know that there is an ink-bottle here," I should be using "know" in the strong sense.

It will appear to some that I have adopted an *unreasonable* attitude toward that statement. There is, however, nothing unreasonable about it. It seems so because one thinks that the statement that here is an ink-bottle *must* have the same status as the statements that the sun is ninety million miles away and that I have a heart and that there will be water in the gorge this afternoon. But this is a *prejudice*.

In saying that I should regard nothing as evidence that there is no ink-bottle here now, I am not *predicting* what I should do if various astonishing things happened. If other members of my family entered this room and, while looking at the top of this desk, declared with apparent sincerity that they see no ink-bottle, I might fall into a swoon or become mad. I *might* even come to believe that there is not and has not been an ink-bottle here. I cannot foretell with certainty how I should react. But if it is *not* a prediction, what is the meaning of my assertion that I should regard nothing as evidence that there is no ink-bottle here?

That assertion describes my *present* attitude toward the statement that here is an ink-bottle. It does not prophesy what my attitude *would* be if various things happened. My present attitude toward that statement is radically different from my present attitude toward those other statements (e.g., that I have a heart).[9] I do *now* admit that certain future occurrences would disprove the latter. Whereas no imaginable future occurrence would be considered by me *now* as proving that there is not an ink-bottle here.

These remarks are not meant to be autobiographical. They are meant to throw light on the common concepts of evidence, proof, and disproof. Every one of us upon innumerable occasions of daily life takes this same attitude toward various statements about physical things, e.g., that here is a torn page, that this dish is broken, that the thermometer reads 70, that no rug is on the floor. Furthermore, the concepts of proof, disproof, doubt, and conjecture *require* us to take this attitude. In order for it to be possible that any statements about physical things should *turn out to be false* it is necessary that some statements about physical things *cannot* turn out to be false.

This will be made clear if we ask ourselves the question, When do we *say* that something turned out to be false? When do we use those words? Someone asks you for a dollar. You

---

[9] The word "attitude" is not very satisfactory, but I cannot think of another noun that would do the trick. By "my attitude" I mean, here, *what I should say and think* if various things were to happen. By "my present* attitude" I mean what I should say and think now, when I imagine those things as happening, in contrast with what I should say and think at some future time if those things actually did happen at that time. It is this distinction that shows that my description of "my present attitude" is not a *prophecy.*

say "There is one in this drawer." You open the drawer and look, but it is perfectly empty. Your statement turned out to be false. This can be said because you *discovered* an empty drawer. It could not be said if it were only probable that the drawer is empty or were still open to question. Would it make sense to say "I had better make sure that it is empty; perhaps there is a dollar in it after all?" Sometimes; but not always. Not if the drawer lies open before your eyes. That remark is the prelude to a search. What search can there be when the emptiness of the drawer confronts you? In certain circumstances there is nothing that you would call "making sure" that the drawer is empty; and likewise nothing that you would call "its turning out to be false" that the drawer is empty. You *made* sure that the drawer is empty. One statement about physical things *turned out to be false* only because you *made sure* of another statement about physical things. The two concepts cannot exist apart. Therefore, it is impossible that *every* statement about physical things *could* turn out to be false.

In a certain important respect some a priori statements and some empirical statements possess the same logical character. The statements that $5 \times 5 = 25$ and that here is an ink-bottle, both lie beyond the reach of doubt. On both, my judgment and reasoning *rests*. If you could somehow undermine my confidence in either, you would not teach me *caution*. You would fill my mind with chaos! I could not even make *conjectures* if you took away those fixed points of certainty; just as a man cannot *try* to climb whose body has no support. A conjecture implies an understanding of what certainty would be. If it is not a certainty that $5 \times 5 = 25$ and that here is an ink-bottle, then I do not understand what it is. You cannot make me doubt either of these statements or treat them as hypotheses. You cannot persuade me that future experience could refute them. With both of them it is perfectly unintelligible to me to speak of a "possibility" that they are false. This is to say that I know both of them to be true, in the strong sense of "know." And I am inclined to think that the strong sense of "know" is what various philosophers have had in mind when they have spoken of "perfect," "metaphysical," or "strict certainty."[10]

It will be thought that I have confused a statement about my "sensations," or my "sense-data," or about the way something *looks* or *appears* to me, with a statement about physical things. It will be thought that the things that I have said about the statement "Here is an ink-bottle" could be true only if that statement is interpreted to mean something like "There appears to me to be an ink-bottle here," i.e., interpreted so as not to assert or imply that any physical thing exists. I wish to make it clear that my statement "Here is an ink-bottle" is *not* to be interpreted in that way. It would be utterly fantastic for me in my present circumstances to say "There appears to me to be an ink-bottle here."

If someone were to call me on the telephone and say that he urgently needed an ink-bottle I should invite him to come here and get this one. If he said that it was extremely urgent that he should obtain one immediately and that he could not afford to waste time going to a place where there might not be one, I should tell him that it is an absolute certainty that there is one here, that nothing could be more certain, that it is something I absolutely guarantee. But if my statement "There is an ink-bottle here" were a statement about my "sensations" or "sense-data," or if it meant that there *appears* to me to be an ink-bottle here or that something here *looks* to me like an ink-bottle, and if that is all that I meant by it—then I should react quite differently to his urgent request. I should say that there is probably an ink-bottle here but that I could not *guarantee* it, and that if he needs one very desperately and at once

[10] Descartes, for example, apparently took as his criterion for something's being "entirely certain" that he could not *imagine* in it the least ground of doubt: ". . . je pensai qu'il fallait . . . que je retasse comme absolument faux tout ce en quoi je pourrais imaginer le moindre doute, afin de voir s'il ne me resterait point après cela quelque chose en ma créance qui fut entièrement indubitable" (*Discourse*, Part IV). And Locke (as previously noted) said of "intuitive knowledge" that one *cannot imagine* a greater certainty, and that it "leaves no room for hesitation, doubt, or examination" (*Essay*, Bk. IV, ch. 2, sec. 1).

then he had better look elsewhere. In short, I wish to make it clear that my statement "Here is an ink-bottle" is strictly about physical things and not about "sensations," "sense-data," or "appearances."[11]

Let us go back to Prichard's remark that we can determine by reflection whether we know something or merely believe it. Prichard would think that "knowledge in the weak sense" is mere belief and not knowledge. This is wrong. But if we let ourselves speak this way, we can then see some justification for Prichard's remark. For then he would be asserting, among other things, that we can determine by reflection whether we know something in the strong sense or in the weak sense. This is not literally true; however, there is this truth in it—that reflection can make us realize that we are *using* "I know it" in the strong (or weak) sense in a particular case. Prichard says that reflection can show us that "our condition is one of knowing" a certain thing, or instead that "our condition is one of believing and not of knowing" that thing. I do not understand what could be meant here by "our condition." The way I should put it is that reflection on *what we should think* if certain things were to happen may make us realize that we should (or should not) call those things "proof" or "evidence" that what we claim to know is not so. I have tried to show that the distinction between strong and weak knowledge does not run parallel to the distinction between a priori and empirical knowledge but cuts across it, i.e., these two kinds of knowledge may be distinguished *within* a priori knowledge and *within* empirical knowledge.

Reflection can make me realize that I am using "know" in the strong sense; but can reflection show me that I *know* something in the strong sense (or in the weak)? It is not easy to state the logical facts here. On the one hand, if I make an

[11] The remainder of the essay is newly written. The original conclusion was wrongly stated. The reader is referred to the following exchange between Richard Taylor and myself, in respect to the original paper: Taylor, "A Note on Knowledge and Belief," *Analysis*, XIII, June 1953; Malcolm, "On Knowledge and Belief," *Analysis*, XIV, March 1954; Taylor, "Rejoinder to Mr. Malcolm," *Analysis*, XIV, March 1954.

assertion of the form "I know that p" it does not follow that p, whether or not I am using "know" in the strong sense. If I have said to someone outside my room "Of course, I know that Freddie is in here," and I am speaking in the strong sense, it does not *follow* that Freddie is where I claim he is. This logical fact would not be altered even if I *realized* that I was using "know" in the strong sense. My reflection on what I should say if . . . cannot show me that I *know* something. From the fact that I should not call anything "evidence" that Freddie is not here, it does not follow that he *is* here; therefore, it does not follow that I *know* he is here.

On the other hand, in an actual case of my using "know" in the strong sense, I cannot envisage a possibility that what I say to be true should turn out to be not true. If I were speaking of *another person's* assertion about something, I *could* think both that he is using "know" in the strong sense and that nonetheless what he claims he knows to be so might turn out to be not so. But *in my own case* I cannot have this conjunction of thoughts, and this is a logical and not a psychological fact. When *I* say that I know something to be so, using "know" in the strong sense, it is unintelligible *to me* (although perhaps not to others) to suppose that anything could prove that it is not so and, therefore, that I do not know it.[12]

---

[12] This is the best summary I can give of what is wrong and right in Prichard's claim that one can determine by reflection whether one knows something or merely believes it. A good part of the ideas in this essay were provoked by conversations with Wittgenstein. A brief and rough account of those talks is to be found in my *Ludwig Wittgenstein: A Memoir* (New York: Oxford University Press, 1958), pp. 87–92. Jaakko Hintikka provides an acute treatment of the topic of "knowing that one knows," with special reference to Prichard's claim. See his *Knowledge and Belief* (Ithaca: Cornell University Press, 1962), ch. 5.

PART TWO

THE "GETTIER PROBLEM"

Edmund L. Gettier

Is Justified True Belief Knowledge?

Various attempts have been made in recent years to state necessary and sufficient conditions for someone's knowing a given proposition. The attempts have often been such that they can be stated in a form similar to the following:[1]

   (a) S knows that P   *IFF*   (i) P is true,
                                  (ii) S believes that P, and
                                  (iii) S is justified in believing that P.

For example, Chisholm has held that the following gives the necessary and sufficient conditions for knowledge:[2]

   (b) S knows that P   *IFF*   (i) S accepts P,
                                  (ii) S has adequate evidence for P, and
                                  (iii) P is true.

From *Analysis,* 23 (1963), 121–123. Reprinted by permission of the author and Basil Blackwell.

[1] Plato seems to be considering some such definition at *Theaetetus* 201, and perhaps accepting one at *Meno* 98.

[2] Roderick M. Chisholm, *Perceiving: a Philosophical Study,* Cornell University Press (Ithaca, New York, 1957), p. 16.

Ayer has stated the necessary and sufficient conditions for knowledge as follows:[3]

> (c) S knows that P   *IFF*   (i) P is true,
> (ii) S is sure that P is true, and
> (iii) S has the right to be sure that P is true.

I shall argue that (a) is false in that the conditions stated therein do not constitute a *sufficient* condition for the truth of the proposition that S knows that P. The same argument will show that (b) and (c) fail if 'has adequate evidence for' or 'has the right to be sure that' is substituted for 'is justified in believing that' throughout.

I shall begin by noting two points. First, in that sense of 'justified' in which S's being justified in believing P is a necessary condition of S's knowing that P, it is possible for a person to be justified in believing a proposition that is in fact false. Secondly, for any proposition P, if S is justified in believing P, and P entails Q, and S deduces Q from P and accepts Q as a result of this deduction, then S is justified in believing Q. Keeping these two points in mind, I shall now present two cases in which the conditions stated in (a) are true for some proposition, though it is at the same time false that the person in question knows that proposition.

Case I

Suppose that Smith and Jones have applied for a certain job. And suppose that Smith has strong evidence for the following conjunctive proposition:

> (d) Jones is the man who will get the job, and Jones has ten coins in his pocket.

[3] A. J. Ayer, *The Problem of Knowledge,* Macmillan (London, 1956), p. 34.

Smith's evidence for (d) might be that the president of the company assured him that Jones would in the end be selected, and that he, Smith, had counted the coins in Jones's pocket ten minutes ago. Proposition (d) entails:

  (e) The man who will get the job has ten coins in his pocket.

Let us suppose that Smith sees the entailment from (d) to (e), and accepts (e) on the grounds of (d), for which he has strong evidence. In this case, Smith is clearly justified in believing that (e) is true.

But imagine, further, that unknown to Smith, he himself, not Jones, will get the job. And, also, unknown to Smith, he himself has ten coins in his pocket. Proposition (e) is then true, though proposition (d), from which Smith inferred (e), is false. In our example, then, all of the following are true: (*i*) (e) is true, (*ii*) Smith believes that (e) is true, and (*iii*) Smith is justified in believing that (e) is true. But it is equally clear that Smith does not *know* that (e) is true; for (e) is true in virtue of the number of coins in Smith's pocket, while Smith does not know how many coins are in Smith's pocket, and bases his belief in (e) on a count of the coins in Jones's pocket, whom he falsely believes to be the man who will get the job.

Case II

Let us suppose that Smith has strong evidence for the following proposition:

  (f) Jones owns a Ford.

Smith's evidence might be that Jones has at all times in the past within Smith's memory owned a car, and always a Ford, and that Jones has just offered Smith a ride while driving a Ford. Let us imagine, now, that Smith has another friend, Brown, of whose whereabouts he is totally ignorant. Smith selects three place names quite at random and constructs the following three propositions:

(g) Either Jones owns a Ford, or Brown is in Boston.
(h) Either Jones owns a Ford, or Brown is in Barcelona.
(i) Either Jones owns a Ford, or Brown is in Brest-Litovsk.

Each of these propositions is entailed by (f). Imagine that Smith realizes the entailment of each of these propositions he has constructed by (f), and proceeds to accept (g), (h), and (i) on the basis of (f). Smith has correctly inferred (g), (h), and (i) from a proposition for which he has strong evidence. Smith is therefore completely justified in believing each of these three propositions. Smith, of course, has no idea where Brown is.

But imagine now that two further conditions hold. First, Jones does *not* own a Ford, but is at present driving a rented car. And secondly, by the sheerest coincidence, and entirely unknown to Smith, the place mentioned in proposition (h) happens really to be the place where Brown is. If these two conditions hold, then Smith does *not* know that (h) is true, even though (*i*) (h) *is* true, (*ii*) Smith does believe that (h) is true, and (*iii*) Smith is justified in believing that (h) is true.

These two examples show that definition (a) does not state a *sufficient* condition for someone's knowing a given proposition. The same cases, with appropriate changes, will suffice to show that neither definition (b) nor definition (c) do so either.

R. M. Chisholm

The Foundation of
Empirical Statements

I shall suggest answers to the following questions which were among those raised in the original prospectus of the Warsaw Colloquy:

It seems to belong to the very content of a scientific statement that it is one which is founded, justified, or valid (*ein begründeter Satz*), and a suggestion that there are scientific statements that are unfounded, gratuitous conjectures seems to imply a contradiction. Yet some methodologists of inductive sciences maintain that neither their basic statements nor their general laws have any foundation (*Begründung*).

What is the object of foundation (justification, validation, legitimization)? Is it the statement itself or possibly its assertion?

If the object of foundation is the assertion of a statement (and thus a kind of human behavior, similar to decision making), could the problem of foundation of statements be viewed in a way similar to the problem of rational decision making?

In what sense, if any, may one speak of the foundation of basic statements in the empirical sciences?

Must the foundation of a statement consist in its derivation from other statements, or may it also consist in its derivation from something that is not a statement (e.g., from a perception)?

From K. Ajdukiewicz (ed.), *The Foundation of Statements and Decisions* (Polish Scientific Publishers, 1965), pp. 111–121. Revised by the author and reprinted with his permission.

Must the concept of a founded statement be thought of as relative or may it be thought of as absolute?

The above quotation contains only part of what was stated in the original prospectus, and I have changed the order of the questions.

I

"What is the object of foundation (justification, validation, legitimization)? Is it the statement itself or possibly its assertion?"

The term "justify" suggests that, if we say a *statement* is justified, what we mean is that a certain kind of human behavior or activity with respect *to* that statement is justified. But what kind of behavior or activity? Not the *assertion* of the statement—if "assertion" is taken to mean the overt utterance, affirmation, or avowal of the statement. For there are many justified statements which we are not justified in overtly asserting; and perhaps there are unjustified statements which, at times, we are justified in overtly asserting. When we say that a statement is justified, what we mean, surely, is that its *acceptance* is justified. What is it, then, to say that a statement is thus acceptable?

A person S may be said to use a statement h as a basis for action if S includes h in his "decision base," if S makes his practical decisions upon the basis, in part, of h. Now some such uses are epistemically *preferable* to others. Thus some statements are such that S's so using them (at a given time t) is preferable to his not so using them (at t); others are such that his not using them is preferable to his using them; and some statements h and i are such that his so using h is preferable to his so using i. Hence we might say that a statement h is *acceptable* for S (at a given time t) if it is false that his *not* so using h (at t) is preferable to his using h (at t). We could add that h is *probable*, or *reasonable*, for S if his so using h is preferable to his not so using h. We could say further that h is *evident* for S, if no statement i is such that S's so using i is preferable to his so using *h*. And we could say, finally, that S *knows h* to be true, if *h* is true, if S believes *h* to be true, and if *h* is thus evident for S.[1]

One advantage of construing evidential, or epistemic, terms in this normative way is the following: we may say that a statement is evident (or probable, or acceptable) for a person without attributing to him any "intuitive insight," "feeling of conviction," or other "cognitive activity."

II

"If the object of foundaton is a kind of human behavior, similar to decision making, could the problem of the foundation of statements be viewed in a way similar to the problem of rational decision making?"

We must solve the problem of the foundation of statements in the *way* in which we must solve the problem of rational decision making: but proper *application* of rational decision theory presupposes proper application of the theory of the justification of statements.

If it were possible to formulate a complete set of rules for rational decision making, these rules would tell us, perhaps among other things, how to decide at any particular time: (1) whether, for any two states of affairs, one would be *better* than the other; (2) whether a given statement is one which, for us, is *evident*, or *probable*, or *acceptable*, or none of these, at that time; (3) whether, with respect to any two statements, the evidence at our disposal at that time (i.e., the set of all those statements which for us are evident at that time) *confirms* one to a higher degree than it confirms the other; and, finally, (4) what we ought to do. Such a set of rules would

[1] I have discussed these epistemic terms in detail in *Theory of Knowledge* (Garden City, N.J., Prentice-Hall, Inc., 1966) and in "The Principles of Epistemic Appraisal," in F. C. Dommeyer (ed.), *Current Philosophical Issues: Essays in Honor of Curt John Ducasse* (Springfield, Ill., Charles C. Thomas, 1966). Compare J. M. Keynes' discussion of probability and preference in *A Treatise on Probability* (London: Macmillan, 1921), p. 307.

constitute a hierarchy in that, in order to apply those that come later on the list, a reasonable man would need first to apply those that come earlier. We may say that ethics or moral philosophy is concerned with (1), epistemology or the theory of knowledge with (2), inductive logic or confirmation theory with (3), and rational decision theory with (4). The *way in which* we should go about formulating these sets of rules is similar in each case: we suppose ourselves able to recognize certain cases which would conform to the rules we are attempting to formulate, and certain other cases which do not conform to them; then, from these sets of cases, we "extract" in Socratic fashion the rules we desire.

III

"In what sense, if any, may one speak of the foundation of basic statements in the empirical sciences?"

First, we must ask: What is a basic statement, and how are we to decide whether there are any? To answer these questions, we must consider what it would be to formulate "rules of evidence."

If we wish to formulate, or make explicit, our rules of evidence, we should proceed as we do in logic when we formulate rules of inference, or in ethics when we formulate rules of action. We suppose that we have at our disposal certain instances which the rules should countenance and other instances which the rules should forbid; and we suppose that by investigating these instances we can formulate criteria which any instance must satisfy if it is to be countenanced, and criteria which any instance must satisfy if it is to be forbidden. To obtain the instances which we should need if we were to formulate rules of evidence, I suggest that we should proceed in the following way.

We should consider certain statements—or beliefs, or hypotheses—which are of the sort that we want to call evident. And we should "examine" these statements by considering, with respect to each of them, what would be a reasonable answer to the following question: "What justification do you have for counting this statement (belief, hypothesis) as one which is evident?" or "What justification do you have for thinking you know this statement is true?" And similarly for statements thought to be merely probable, and statements thought to be merely acceptable.

There are philosophers who will point out, with respect to some statements which are quite obviously true, that questions concerning their justification or evidence "do not arise," for (they will say) to express a doubt concerning such statements is (somehow) to "violate the rules of our language." To these philosophers we may point out that our questions need not be taken to express any doubts or to indicate an attitude of scepticism. They are not challenges and they do not imply or presuppose that there is any ground for doubting, or for suspecting, the statements with which they are concerned; they seek only to elicit information.[2] When Aristotle considered an invalid mood and asked himself "What is wrong with this?" he was trying to learn; he need not have been suggesting to himself that perhaps nothing was wrong with the mood.

It should also be noted that when we ask, concerning some evident statement, "What justification do you have for counting this statement as one which is evident?" or "What justification do you have for thinking you know that this statement is one which is true?" we are not asking what procedures might *further confirm* the statement. We are supposing that the statement is one which is evident, and we are attempting to discover the nature of its evidence.

In many instances the answers to our questions could take

[2] This objection applies also to Leonard Nelson's statement: "If one asks whether one possesses objectively valid cognitions at all, one thereby presupposes that the objectivity of cognition is questionable at first" (*Socratic Method and Critical Philosophy*, New Haven 1949, p. 190). One of the unfortunate consequences of the work of Descartes, Russell, and Husserl is the widely accepted supposition that questions about the justification for counting evident statements *as* evident must be *challenges*, or expressive of *doubts*. The objections to this supposition were clearly put by Meinong (cf. Volume II of his *Gesammelte Abhandlungen*, Leipzig 1913, p. 191).

the following form: "What justifies me in counting it as evident that *a* is *F* is the fact that (i) it is evident that *b* is *G* and (ii) if it is evident that *b* is *G* then it is evident that *a* is *F*." (Or, "What justifies me in saying that I know that *a* is *F* is the fact that (i) I know that *b* is *G* and (ii) if I know that *b* is *G*, then I know that *a* is *F*.") For example, "What makes it evident that he has that disorder is the fact that it is evident that he has these symptoms, and if it is evident that he has these symptoms then it is evident that he has that disorder." Such a reply has two parts. First, we say that our justification for counting one statement as evident is the fact that a certain other statement is evident. And secondly, we offer what may be called a "rule of evidence"; for we make a statement which says that if a statement of the second sort is evident then a statement of the first sort is also evident. One could say, of the rule, that it tells us that one statement *confers evidence* upon another statement.

Such a reply to our questions would shift the burden of justification from one statement to another. For we may now ask, "What justifies you in counting it as evident that *b* is *G*?" (or "What justifies you in thinking you know that *b* is *G*?").[3] And to this question we may receive again an answer of the first sort: "What justifies me in counting it as evident that *b* is *G* is the fact that (i) it is evident that *c* is *H* and (ii) if it is evident that *c* is *H* then it is evident that *b* is *G*." ("What justifies me in counting it as evident that he has these symptoms is the fact that it is evident that his temperature is high, his face is flushed . . .") How long can we continue in this way?

Let us note that our replies may take a slightly different form from that just considered. The phrase "it is evident that" may be omitted from the first part, and from the first part of the second part, of the reply, leaving us with: "What justifies me in counting it as evident that *a* is *F*, is the fact that (i)

---

[3] We may also ask, of course, for a justification of the rule of evidence; the problems which such questions involve are beyond the scope of the present paper. Note that the reply described above does not say that the rule of evidence is evident.

b is G and (ii) if b is G then it is evident that a is F." In some cases, we may say that the fact that it is *evident* that b is G is implicit in such a reply, but in others, according to what I take to be the views of some philosophers, it may not be.

If we say, as I think we should, that there are some statements which are evident and that the interrogation just described should involve neither a vicious circle nor an infinite regress, then we are committed to saying that there are "basic statements."

Let us suppose that, in the course of describing the justification of some statement, we have made a statement, "a is F," and we are now confronted with the question: "What justification do you have for counting the statement that a is F as one which is evident?" I suggest that the statement that a is F could be said to be a "basic statement" if it would be reasonable to answer the question in either of the following ways:

(1) "What justifies me in counting it as evident that a is F is simply the fact that a is F."

(2) "The statement that a is F cannot properly be said to be evident (or to be non-evident) and therefore the question 'What is your justification for counting it as evident that a is F?' cannot arise."

In the first case, we have a statement which is made evident by the fact that it is true; in the second, we have a statement which is not itself evident (or which "cannot properly be said" to be evident) but which may, all the same, confer evidence upon other statements. Thus the first suggests a prime mover which moves itself, the second a prime mover unmoved. In the present case, I believe, the two descriptions differ only in terminology. The issues which are involved in saying this may be seen if we consider certain particular "basic statements."

One advantage in describing "basic statements" in one or the other of the present two ways is that our discussion neither touches upon "certainty" and "incorrigibility" nor becomes entangled in the issues to which these misleading terms sometimes give rise.

IV

"Must the foundation of a statement consist in its derivation
from other statements, or may it also consist in its derivation
from something that is not a statement (e.g., from a perception)?"

Let us first ask: Are perceptual statements—statements expressing what we perceive—"basic" in either of the senses just
described?

To justify the statement that Mr. Smith is here, one may say
"I see that he is here." But "I see that he is here" is not a "basic
statement" in either sense described. In reply to the question,
"What is your justification for counting it as evident that it is
Mr. *Smith* whom you see?" a reasonable man would *not* say,
"What justifies me in counting it as evident that it is Mr.
Smith is simply the fact that it *is* Mr. Smith." Nor would he
say, "The statement that it is Mr. Smith whom I see is not a
statement which can properly be said to be evident." He would
say, instead, something like this: "(It is evident that:) Mr.
Smith is a tall man with dark glasses; I see such a man; no one
else satisfying that description would be in *this* room now . . .
Etc." And each of these statements in turn, including "I see
such a man," would be defended by appeal to still other statements. And similarly for any other perceptual statement. If
this is so, perception does not yield any "basic statements" in
either of the two senses of that term we have described.

There are philosophers who might say, "What justifies me in
counting it as evident that Mr. Smith is here (or that I see Mr.
Smith) is simply my present experience; but the experience
itself cannot be said to be evident, much less to have evidence
conferred upon it." With this reply they have supposed themselves able to circumvent some of the more difficult questions
of the theory of knowledge.[4] Yet the reply seems clearly to

[4] See Leonard Nelson's *Über das sogenannte Erkenntnisproblem*,
Göttingen 1930, reprinted from *Abhandlungen der Fries'schen Schule*,
Vol. II, Göttingen 1908; esp. pp. 479–485, 502–503, 521–524, 528.
Compare also his "The Impossibility of the 'Theory of Knowledge'" in
Socratic Method and Critical Philosophy, New Haven 1949, esp. pp.
190–192.

make room for further questioning. Thus one may ask, "What justifies you in counting it as evident that your experience is of such a sort that experiences of that sort make it evident to you that Mr. Smith is here, or that you see that Mr. Smith is here?" And to this question, one could reasonably reply in the way described above.

It must be conceded, I think, that the only empirical "basic statements," in our present sense of the term, are certain psychological statements about oneself. For example, any one of the following statements *may* be so interpreted that it is "basic" in one or the other of our two senses: "I seem to remember having seen that man before," "That looks green," "This tastes bitter," "I believe that Socrates is mortal," and "I hope that the peace will continue." Let us consider the first of these.

The statement "I seem to remember having seen that man before" is one to which we may appeal in justifying some other statement. Thus part of my justification for counting it as evident that I have been among these people before may be the fact that I seem to remember having seen that man before; and if *you* say "I seem to remember having seen him before," part of my justification for counting it as evident that you and I seem to remember the same thing is the fact that *I* seem to remember having seen him before. How, then, shall we deal with the question "What justification do you have for counting it as evident that you have seen that man before?" It seems clear to me that we must choose between the two alternatives I have described, and hence that the statement in question is one which is "basic."

(1) We may say, "What justifies me in counting it as evident that I seem to remember having seen that man before is simply the fact that I *do* seem to remember having seen him before." In this case, we have justified a statement simply by reiterating it. This type of justification, if I am not mistaken, is never appropriate to empirical statements which are not psychological; and if what I have said above is correct, it is never ap-

propriate to ordinary perceptual statements. We should
also note that such a justification presupposes that the
statement justified is a *true* statement.

(2) We may say what many philosophers would now prefer to say: "The fact that I seem to remember having
seen that man before is not something which can properly be said to be *evident;* hence the question 'What
justifies you in counting it as evident?' is not a question
which can arise."

In defence of the second way of putting the matter, one
may point out that, ordinarily, people never do apply such
terms as "evident" to such statements as "I seem to remember
having seen that man before."[5] (But from this fact alone, it
would be a mistake to infer that "evident" cannot correctly
be applied to such statements.) One may also point out that
seeming to remember is not accompanied by a second-order
consciousness, or insight, which "illuminates" one's seeming
to remember.[6] (But to infer from this that it cannot be said
to be evident to me that I seem to remember would be to
presuppose that a statement cannot be said to be evident unless it concerns something which is revealed by a special kind
of consciousness or illumination; and, according to what was
said at the end of Section I above, such a presupposition is
gratuitous.) It seems clear to me that this second way of
formulating our basic statements differs only verbally from
the first.[7]

[5] Compare L. Wittgenstein, *Philosophical Investigations,* Oxford 1953,
p. 89e: "It can't be said of me at all (except perhaps as a joke) that I
know I am in pain. What is it supposed to mean—except perhaps that
I *am* in pain?"

[6] "We do not ask for one torch to help us to see and another to help
us to recognize what we see" (Gilbert Ryle, *The Concept of Mind,*
London 1949, p. 162).

[7] Some of Ajdukiewicz's *Sinnregeln,* but, I believe, not all of them,
could be regarded as telling us what statements are "basic" in our present
sense; see K. Ajdukiewicz, "Sprache und Sinn," *Erkenntnis,* Vol. IV,
1934, p. 100 ff. A similar remark may be made of the simple "acceptance
rules" which Carnap formulates in "Truth and Confirmation"; see esp.

If the "basic statements" of empirical knowledge are psychological statements about oneself, then the "basic statements" of the empirical sciences must be found among those statements which, for each empirical scientist, are basic for him. How are we to show that "objective" science can thus be "subjectively" based? Only, I think, by formulating rules of evidence which will state the conditions under which statements which are subjective may be said to confer evidence upon statements which are not. I can state possible examples of such rules; but the task of deciding whether these, or any other, rules are adequate has yet to be carried out.

Let us recall that we have distinguished the concepts of a statement being *evident*, a statement being *probable* (more probable than not), and a statement being *acceptable*. If a statement is evident it is probable, but not conversely; and if a statement is probable it is acceptable, but not conversely.

Rules taking the following form might be described as epistemically liberal, or latitudinarian:

"For any subject S, if it is evident to S that S seems to remember that *a* was *F*, then it is evident to S that *a* was *F*."

"For any subject S, if it is evident to S that S thinks S perceives that *a* is *F*, then it is evident to S that *a* is *F*."

If we are to decide to formulate our "basic propositions" in the second of the two ways described, then we should omit the first occurrence of "it is evident to S that" in each of these rules.

The rules may be made more rigid by replacing the second occurrence of "evident" in each of them by "probable," and even more rigid by replacing it by "acceptable." And if the rules turn out to be still too liberal, as perhaps they may, we can consider such possibilities as these:

"For any subject S, if it is evident to S that S seems to remember that *a* was *F*, then it is evident (probable, acceptable) to S that *a* was *F*, provided that the statement that he *does* remember that *a* was *F* is not disconfirmed by the set of all

pp. 124–125, in the version of that article in H. Feigl and W. S. Sellars, eds., *Readings in Philosophical Analysis*, New York, 1949.

the other statements expressing what it is evident to S that he seems to remember."

"For any subject S, if it is evident to S that S thinks S perceives that *a* is *F*, then it is evident (probable, acceptable) to S that *a* is *F*, provided that the statement that he *does* perceive that *a* is *F* is not disconfirmed by the set of all the other statements expressing either what it is evident to S that he seems to remember or what it is evident to S that he seems to perceive."

Perhaps the expression "other statements" is better replaced by "statements not logically implied by the statement that *a* is *F*."

The rules of inductive logic, or confirmation theory, may be construed in this way, as telling us the conditions under which sets of evident statements may be said to confer probability upon statements which are not evident. We may find that there are certain statements in the empirical sciences which we wish to count as evident, but which we cannot count as evident unless inductive logic includes, in addition to rules of probability, certain rules of evidence. An inductive rule of evidence would be a rule specifying conditions under which confirmation by a set of evident statements could confer evidence upon a statement that is not entailed by that set.

We can say, of our "basic statements," that if they are evident they are also true. But our rules do not guarantee, with respect to other statements, that if *they* are evident, then they, too, are true. If it is possible that some statements are both evident and false, then we must take further steps in order to deal with a problem that has been pointed out by Edmund L. Gettier.[8] We had said that a person S *knows* a statement *h* to be true provided that *h* is true, S believes *h* to be true, and *h* is evident for S. But Mr. Gettier notes the possibility of this type of situation. Suppose "I see a sheep in the field" is a *false* statement *i* which happens to be evident for S. We may imagine, say, that S takes a dog to be a sheep, but does so under

[8] Edmund L. Gettier, "Is Justified True Belief Knowledge?" *Analysis*, 23 (1963), 121–123. [Pp. 35–38 of the present volume. Ed.]

conditions which are such that, according to our rules of evidence, if a man takes anything to be a sheep under those conditions, then it is evident to him that he sees a sheep. Since "I see a sheep in the field" is false, it will not be a statement that S knows to be true. But since it is evident, then so, too, of course, is "There is a sheep in the field" (h). Suppose, then, that there happens to *be* a sheep in the field, but one that S knows nothing about. This situation, clearly, would not warrant our saying that S *knows* that there is a sheep in the field. But the conditions of our definition of knowledge are satisfied, for "There is a sheep in the field" is a statement h which is such that h is true, S believes h to be true, and h is evident for S. If this type of situation is in fact possible, we must choose between two courses. We could make our criteria of the evident more rigid in order to make sure that they are not satisfied by the "I see a sheep in the field" of our example or by any other false statement. Or we might qualify our definition of knowledge in order to make sure that in this instance it is not satisfied by "S knows that there is a sheep in the field." The former course would have the effect of restricting our knowledge to the "basic statements" we have discussed. And so we need a definition of "S knows that h is true" which will be adequate to our concept of knowledge but will not entitle us to say that the h of our example ("There is a sheep in the field") is known to be true by S.

Let us say that e *makes h evident* for S provided only: S believes that e is true; e is evident for S; and necessarily any subject for whom e is evident is also one for whom h is evident. The h of our example is made evident for S by a statement e that is false ("I see a sheep in the field"). Hence we may be tempted to qualify our definition of knowledge by adding to it: "What makes h evident for S does not make any falsehood evident for S." But this would not be enough. The h of our example is also made evident by many statements other than e (e.g., by h itself, by the disjunction of h and e, by the conjunction of h or e with any other evident statement, by the result of disjoining e with the conjunction of h and any statement whatever) and if any of *these* statements is such as to make no falsehood evident, then the revised definition of knowledge would also be satisfied by the h of our example. Should we, then, qualify the definition of knowledge by saying: "Nothing that makes h evident for S makes evident any falsehood for S"? This would exclude too much. Consider some statement k that the S of our example does know to be true: this is made evident for S by the conjunction, e and k; but the conjunction, e and k, makes the false statement e evident for S; and therefore the proposed qualification would require us to say that S does not know k to be true.

Of the various statements that do thus make h evident for S, some are more central than others. Let us say that a statement c is *central* to what makes h evident for S, provided only this condition holds: anything that makes h evident for S and does not entail h is equivalent to a disjunction of mutually consistent statements one of which entails c. And let us say that a statement v is *nondefectively evident* for S, provided only that v is evident for S and is equivalent to a conjunction of statements each of which is such that nothing that is central to what makes it evident for S makes evident any statement that is false. I suggest that everything we know to be true is thus nondefectively evident for us, but the h of our example is not nondefectively evident for S. If this is correct, then we may revise our definition of knowledge by adding the one word "nondefectively": S *knows* that h is true, provided only that h is true, S believes that h is true, and h is nondefectively evident for S.

V

"Must the concept of a founded statement be thought of as relative, or may it be thought of as absolute?"

The foundation of statements may be said to be "relative" in the sense that, for any statement h, it is possible for h to be evident (or probable, or acceptable) for one man and not for another. But our rules may be said to be "absolute" in the sense that they formulate conditions of being evident (or probable, or acceptable) which hold for all men. Thus we have used the phrase "For any subject S."

What if someone were to propose an alternative set of rules—by beginning with cases quite different from those with which we began? And suppose we find that we can reach no agreement with him concerning any of those cases which, at the outset, are to be counted as instances of what is evident, or probable, or acceptable. Shall we say that at most one of two such sets of conflicting rules is valid or correct? I am afraid I cannot answer this ancient question—beyond saying that what may be said about the correctness or validity of rules of evidence should also hold, *mutatis mutandis,* of the rules of logic, ethics, and the theory of rational decision.

Keith Lehrer

Knowledge, Truth and Evidence

If a man is not completely justified in believing something, then he does not know it. On the other hand, if what he believes is true and he is completely justified in believing it, then it would seem that he knows it. This suggests that we may analyze the statement

S knows h

as the conjunction of

(i) h is true,
(ii) S believes h, and
(iii) S is completely justified in believing h.

Professor Gettier has recently shown this analysis to be defective.[1] To meet the kind of counterexample he has formu-

From *Analysis*, 25 (1965), 168–175. Reprinted by permission of the author and Basil Blackwell.

[1] Edmund L. Gettier, "Is Justified True Belief Knowledge?" *Analysis*, Vol. 23, pp. 121–123. [Pp. 35–38 of the present volume. Ed.] Mr. Michael Clark, "Knowledge and Grounds: A Comment on Mr. Gettier's Paper," *Analysis*, Vol. 24, pp. 46–47, suggests that S's belief must be fully grounded. Defects in Mr. Clark's suggestion have been pointed out by John Turk Saunders and Narayan Champawat, "Mr. Clark's Definition of 'Knowledge,'" *Analysis*, Vol. 25, pp. 8–9, and Ernest Sosa, "The

lated, it is necessary to add some fourth condition to the proposed analysis.

The primary concern of my paper will be to solve the problem that Professor Gettier has raised. However, before turning to that problem, I wish to make a few remarks concerning the third condition to avoid misunderstanding. Firstly, a person may be completely justified in believing something which is in fact false. We shall consider examples of this shortly.

Secondly, though there may be some cases in which a person is completely justified in believing something in the absence of any evidence to justify his belief, the analysis offered here is intended to apply only to those cases in which a person must have evidence to be completely justified in believing what he does. There are a number of ways in which a person who has evidence for what he believes may nevertheless fail to be completely justified in believing what he does. A person may, for example, fail to be completely justified simply because the evidence that he has is not adequate to completely justify his belief.

Moreover, if a person has evidence adequate to completely justify his belief, he may still fail to be completely justified in believing what he does because his belief is not *based on* that evidence. What I mean by saying that a person's belief is not based on certain evidence is that he would not appeal to that evidence to justify his belief. For example, a detective who rejects the truthful testimony of a reliable eye-witness to a

Analysis of 'Knowledge that P,' " *Analysis*, Vol. 25, pp. 1–3. Saunders and Champawat conclude that it is a mistake to believe that some set of conditions are individually necessary and jointly sufficient for knowledge. Unless there is some error in the analysis of knowledge I propose at the end of this paper, I will have shown that there is no reason to accept their conclusion. Sosa also proposes an analysis of knowledge in his paper to meet the difficulty Gettier has raised. But I believe this analysis is defective and fails to solve the problem. For my reasons, see footnote 3 below. I have been fortunate enough to discuss this problem with a number of philosophers, and I am indebted to many for the ideas contained in this paper. I am especially indebted to Professors Roderick Chisholm, Gilbert Harman, David Kaplan, and Edmund Gettier for their refutations of my mistakes.

crime, but accepts the lying testimony of an ignorant meddler, when both tell him that Brentano committed the crime, would fail to be completely justified in believing this. For his belief is not based on the adequate evidence supplied by the truthful eye-witness but is instead based on the inadequate evidence supplied by an ignorant man.

Again, even if a person has evidence adequate to completely justify his belief and his belief is based on that evidence, he may still fail to be completely justified in believing what he does. For he may be unable to provide any plausible line of reasoning to show how one could reach the conclusion he believes from the evidence that he has. For example, a detective who has a complicated mass of evidence that is conclusive evidence for the conclusion that Little Nelson is the leader of the gang might reach that conclusion from his evidence by what is nothing more than a lucky guess. Imagine that the only line of reasoning he can supply to show how he reached his conclusion is entirely fallacious or that he can supply none. In that case the detective would not be completely justified in believing what he does.

Finally, a man may be completely justified in believing something but fail to believe it because he does not appreciate the strength of his evidence. In this case, the man lacks knowledge because of a lack of belief rather than of justification for belief.

With these qualifications having been noted, let us now turn to the problem of amending the proposed analysis of knowledge to meet the counterexample Professor Gettier has presented against it.

Gettier argues that if a person is completely justified in believing P and he deduces H from P, and believes H on the basis of P, then he is completely justified in believing H. Given this principle we can construct a counterexample to the proposed analysis. Imagine the following: I see two men enter my office whom I know to be Mr. Nogot and Mr. Havit. I have just seen Mr. Nogot depart from a Ford, and he tells me that he has just purchased the car. Indeed, he shows me a certificate that states that he owns the Ford. Moreover, Mr. Nogot is a friend of mine whom I know to be honest and reliable. On the basis of this evidence, I would be completely justified in believing

P1: Mr. Nogot, who is in my office, owns a Ford.

I might deduce from this that

H: Someone in my office owns a Ford.

I would then be completely justified in believing H. However, imagine that, contrary to my evidence, Mr. Nogot has deceived me and that he does not own a Ford. Moreover, imagine that Mr. Havit, the only other man I see in my room, does own a Ford, though I have no evidence that he (or I) owns a Ford. In this case, which I shall hereafter refer to as *case one*, though H is true, and I am completely justified in my belief that it is true, I do not know that it is true.[2] For, the reason that H is true is that Mr. Havit owns a Ford, and I have no evidence that this is so.

We have said that a person is completely justified in believing a statement only if he has adequate evidence to completely justify his belief and his belief is based on that evidence. It might seem that since

P1: Mr. Nogot, who is in my office, owns a Ford

is false, it is also false that I have evidence adequate to completely justify my belief that

H: Someone in my office owns a Ford.

But this is incorrect. Leaving P1 aside, I have adequate evidence for H that consists entirely of *true* statements. The evidence is that which I have for P1, namely, that I see Mr. Nogot in my office, have just seen him get out of a Ford, etc.

---

[2] My examples differ slightly from Gettier's.

All these things are true and provide evidence adequate to completely justify my believing H. Moreover, my belief that H is true is based on that evidence, though it is also based on P1.

Nevertheless, it might seem reasonable to add to the proposed analysis of knowledge a fourth condition to the effect that if a person knows something, then his belief is not based on any false statements. Thus in addition to the previous three conditions, we would add the condition

  (iv) It is not the case that S believes h on the basis of any false statement.

But this condition is much too strong. Imagine that case one is modified so that in addition to the evidence that I have for believing that Mr. Nogot owns a Ford, I have equally strong evidence for believing that Mr. Havit owns a Ford. Moreover, imagine that my belief that someone in my office owns a Ford is based both on the false statement

  P1: Mr. Nogot, who is in my office, owns a Ford

and on the true statement

  P2: Mr. Havit, who is in my office, owns a Ford.

In this case, which I shall refer to as *case two*, it would be correct to say that I know

  H: Someone in my office owns a Ford.

But condition (iv) is not satisfied, and therefore must be rejected.[3]

---

[3] Mr. Sosa, *op. cit.*, pp. 4–8, attempts to meet the difficulty that Gettier has raised, by adding the following condition to the analysis of knowledge: if S's belief is based substantially on the report that h or e_i (e_i is part of the evidence S has for h), then the reporter knows that h or e_i. This condition will fail to be satisfied in a slightly modified version of

I know H in case two, because in addition to the evidence that I have for the false statement P1 which entails (but is not entailed by) H, I also have evidence for the true statement P2 which entails H, and this additional evidence is adequate to completely justify my believing H. This suggests that the following condition might be more satisfactory than the one we have just considered:

(iv a) If S is completely justified in believing any false statement p which entails (but is not entailed by) h, then S has evidence adequate to completely justify his believing h in addition to the evidence he has for p.

This condition is not satisfied in case one. In that case I do not have evidence adequate to completely justify my believing

H: Someone in my office owns a Ford

---

case two. Imagine that my belief that H is true is based on the report by Mr. Nogot that he owns a Ford, that this report is in fact true, but that this is *not* something that Mr. Nogot knows to be true. Mr. Nogot thinks that he does not own a Ford, but he has, unknown to himself, become a Ford owner. On the other hand, Mr. Havit reports knowingly that he, Havit, owns a Ford. In this case, my belief that H is true is based substantially on the unknowing report of Mr. Nogot. For, my belief that H is true is based as much on P1 as it is on P2. Thus, Mr. Sosa's condition is too strong, because it would not be satisfied in this case even though I do know that H is true. Moreover, the condition is also too weak. Imagine that in case one the evidence that I have for P1 does not involve the report of anyone and that P1 is false. For example, imagine that I have seen Mr. Nogot drive a Ford on many occasions and that I now see him drive away in it. Moreover, imagine that he leaves his wallet at my house and that I, being curious, examine its contents. Therein I discover a certificate asserting that Mr. Nogot owns the Ford I have just seen him drive away. This would supply me with evidence, consisting of true statements, which would completely justify my believing P1, and, therefore, H. But now imagine that, as in case one, P1 is false (due to some legal technicality) and P2 is true, though I have no evidence for P2. In this case, I do not know H, but all of Mr. Sosa's requirements for knowledge might well be met. Therefore, the analysis is too weak.

in addition to the evidence I have for the false statement

P1: Mr. Nogot, who is in my office, owns a Ford

which entails H. Thus, condition (iv a) will yield the correct result that I do not know H in case one. So far so good, but now let us consider case two.

In case two, I know

H: Someone in my office owns a Ford

because I have adequate evidence for the true statement

P2: Mr. Havit, who is in my office, owns a Ford.

However, in this case I also have adequate evidence for the false statement

P3: Mr. Nogot and Mr. Havit, who are in my office, own Fords

and, consequently, I would be completely justified in believing P3. But P3 entails H, and, unfortunately, I have no evidence for H in addition to the evidence that I have for P3. The only evidence that I have for H is precisely the evidence that I have for the false statement P3 which entails H. Thus, condition (iv a) would yield the incorrect result that I do not know H in case two, and, consequently, this condition must also be rejected.

To avoid this difficulty, we could formulate a condition to the effect that if a person is completely justified in believing a false statement which entails a true one, then some part of his evidence must be adequate to completely justify his believing the true statement but not adequate to completely justify his believing the false statement. In case two, the evidence that I have for

P2: Mr. Havit, who is in my office, owns a Ford

is adequate to completely justify my believing the true statement

H: Someone in my office owns a Ford

but not adequate to completely justify my believing the false statements

P1: Mr. Nogot, who is in my office, owns a Ford

or

P3: Mr. Nogot and Mr. Havit, who are in my office, own Fords.

The fourth condition would read as follows:

(iv b) If S is completely justified in believing any false statement p which entails (but is not entailed by) h, then S has some evidence adequate to completely justify his believing h but not adequate to completely justify his believing p.

This condition will not be satisfied in case one, because in that case I do not have any evidence that would be adequate to completely justify my believing

H: Someone in my office owns a Ford

that would not completely justify my believing

P1: Mr. Nogot, who is in my office, owns a Ford.

This is a desired result, because I do not know H in that case. But this condition must also be rejected.

The reason is that there are statements which a person might be completely justified in believing in the absence of any evidence to support them. I shall defend the claim that there are such statements presently, but let us assume for the moment that R is such a statement.[4] Moreover, assume that R is false. Now, imagine the following. I have adequate evidence to completely justify my believing

P2: Mr. Havit, who is in my office, owns a Ford

but do not have any evidence for P1, and again P2 is true. In this case, which I shall refer to as *case three*, we may suppose that the evidence I have for P2 is irrelevant to R and that I am completely justified in believing the conjunction of P2 and R. However, this conjunction is a false statement, because R is false, and it entails

H: Someone in my office owns a Ford.

Thus I have no evidence adequate to completely justify my believing H that is not also adequate to completely justify my believing the false statement which is the conjunction of P2 and R and which entails H. So, condition (iv b) would not be satisfied in this case, even though I know that H is true.[5]

The proof that there are statements which a person is completely justified in believing in the absence of any evidence to support them is this. Assume that evidence e is adequate to completely justify my believing h. In that case, the statement that e materially implies h is one that I am completely justified in believing in the absence of any evidence to support it or its denial.

[4] An example of R, that is, a statement a person might be completely justified in believing in the absence of any evidence to support it or its denial, is the following R: If I place twelve marbles into an urn on my desk (without observing their colour), draw out eleven at random which I observe to be black, replace the eleven marbles in the urn and repeat this procedure thirty times with the same results, then all of the marbles in the urn are black. The evidence that I have for P2 is irrelevant to R, R might be false, and I would be completely justified in believing the conjunction of P2 and R if I were completely justified in believing each conjunct.

[5] This argument was suggested to me by David Kaplan.

To solve the problem it is essential to notice what would result were I to suppose in the cases we have considered that those statements are false which are in fact false and which entail H. For example, if I were to suppose in case one that

P1: Mr. Nogot, who is in my office, owns a Ford

is false, I would not in that case be justified in appealing to the evidence that I have for P1 to justify my believing H. Consequently, I would not be completely justified in believing H in case one if I were to suppose that P1 is false.

On the other hand, if I were to suppose in case two that P1 is false, we would not obtain the same result. For in that case I have adequate evidence for P2 as well as P1, and, consequently, I would still be justified in believing H on the basis of the evidence I have for P2. Moreover, even if I were to suppose that the conjunction of P1 and P2 is false in case two, I would still be completely justified in believing H. For I could reason as follows. To suppose that the conjunction of P1 and P2 is false, I need only suppose that one of the conjuncts is false. If P1 is false, then I would be completely justified in believing H on the basis of the evidence that I have for P2. If P2 is false, then I would be completely justified in believing H on the basis of the evidence that I have for P1. Therefore, even if I were to suppose that the conjunction is false, since I am not thereby committed to supposing that both conjuncts are false, I would still be completely justified in believing H.

Similarly, in case three I would be completely justified in believing H even if I were to suppose the conjunction of P2 and R is false. For I could reason that to suppose the conjunction is false does not commit me to supposing that both conjuncts are false, and, consequently, I may suppose that R is false and P2 is true. I would then be completely justified in believing H on the basis of the evidence I have for P2.[6]

---

[6] I am assuming in both cases two and three that, though I suppose that certain statements are false, which are false, and which entail H,

We now have the following results. In case one I would not be completely justified in believing H if I were to suppose that P1 is false, but in case two I would be completely justified in believing H even if I were to suppose that P1 is false or if I were to suppose that the conjunction of P1 and P2 is false, and in case three I would be completely justified in believing H even if I were to suppose that the conjunction of R and P2 is false. Since I know H to be true in case two and three but not in case one, I propose the following as a fourth condition in the analysis of knowledge:

(iv c) If S is completely justified in believing any false statement p which entails (but is not entailed by) h, then S would be completely justified in believing h even if S were to suppose that p is false.[7]

This condition, as we have seen, is satisfied in case two and three but not in case one. Consequently, by adding it to our analysis of knowledge, we gain the result that our analysis is satisfied in just those cases in which we have knowledge and not otherwise.

In connection with these remarks, it is important to notice certain facts about the role of supposition in justification. In the first place, a man need not believe what he supposes to be true. I may suppose that something is true (perhaps to comply with the wishes of another) and examine the consequence of such a supposition without believing what I suppose. I may

---

I do not suppose anything else (not entailed by the former suppositions) which would be adverse to justifying my belief that H is true.

[7] The subjunctive character of this condition allows for some ambiguity concerning what S is to suppose other than the falsity of p and how his beliefs might be altered when the antecedent of this condition is satisfied. We can eliminate some of this ambiguity by stipulating that the expression "if S were to suppose that p is false" is short for "if S were to suppose that p is false but neither suppose anything else (except what is entailed by the supposition that p is false) which is adverse to justifying his belief that h is true, nor alter his beliefs in any way which is adverse to such justification."

suppose that P1 is false and examine the consequences of that supposition without believing what I suppose. Secondly, a man need not count as evidence all that he supposes. I may suppose that the conjunction of P1 and P2 is false without counting that as evidence that I have. For my supposition might be entirely unjustified. Thirdly, suppositions which are neither believed nor counted as evidence may still have the role of preventing a person from appealing to certain evidence that he has to justify his beliefs. Thus, were I to suppose in case one that P1 is false, I would not believe this nor would I count it as evidence that I have, but that supposition would prevent me from appealing to the evidence I have for P1 to justify my believing H.

With these qualifications, I propose the conjunction of conditions (i), (ii), (iii) and (iv c) as an analysis of knowledge.

Alvin I. Goldman

A Causal Theory of Knowing*

Since Edmund L. Gettier pointed out a certain important inadequacy of the traditional analysis of "S knows that p," several attempts have been made to correct that analysis.[1] In this paper I shall offer still another analysis (or sketch of an analysis) of "S knows that p," one which will avert Gettier's problem. My concern will be with knowledge of empirical propositions only. Although certain elements in my theory would be relevant to the analysis of knowledge of nonempirical

From *The Journal of Philosophy*, 64, 12 (June 22, 1967), 357–372. Revised by the author. Reprinted by permission of the author and *The Journal of Philosophy*.

* I wish to thank members of the University of Michigan Philosophy Department, several of whom made helpful comments on earlier versions of this paper.

[1] "Is Justified True Belief Knowledge?" *Analysis*, XXIII.6, ns 96 (June 1963): 121–123. [Pp. 35–38 of the present volume. Ed.] New analyses have been proposed by Michael Clark, "Knowledge and Grounds: A Comment on Mr. Gettier's Paper," *Analysis*, XXIV.2, ns 98 (December 1963): 46–48; Ernest Sosa, "The Analysis of 'Knowledge That P,'" *Analysis*, XXV.1, ns 103 (October 1964): 1–3; and Keith Lehrer, "Knowledge, Truth, and Evidence," *Analysis*, XXV.5, ns 105 (April 1965): 168–175. [Pp. 55–66 of the present volume. Ed.] An outline of a causal theory of knowing appears in Robert Binkley, "A Theory of Practical Reason," *The Philosophical Review*, LXXIV.4, ns 412 (October 1965): 423–448 (cf. pp. 432–435).

truths, my theory is not intended to apply to knowledge of nonempirical truths.

Consider an abbreviated version of Gettier's second counterexample to the traditional analysis. Smith believes

(q) Jones owns a Ford

and has very strong evidence for it. Smith's evidence might be that Jones has owned a Ford for many years and that Jones has just offered Smith a ride while driving a Ford. Smith has another friend, Brown, of whose whereabouts he is totally ignorant. Choosing a town quite at random, however, Smith constructs the proposition

(p) Either Jones owns a Ford or Brown is in Barcelona.

Seeing that q entails p, Smith infers that p is true. Since he has adequate evidence for q, he also has adequate evidence for p. But now suppose that Jones does *not* own a Ford (he was driving a rented car when he offered Smith a ride), but, quite by coincidence, Brown happens to be in Barcelona. This means that p is true, that Smith believes p, and that Smith has adequate evidence for p. But Smith does not know p.

A variety of hypotheses might be made to account for Smith's not knowing p. Michael Clark, for example, points to the fact that q is false, and suggests this as the reason why Smith cannot be said to know p. Generalizing from this case, Clark[2] argues that, for S to know a proposition, each of S's grounds for it must be *true*, as well as his grounds for his grounds, etc. I shall make another hypothesis to account for the fact that Smith cannot be said to know p, and I shall generalize this into a new analysis of "S knows that p."

Notice that what *makes* p true is the fact that Brown is in Barcelona, but that this fact has nothing to do with Smith's believing p. That is, there is no *causal* connection between the fact that Brown is in Barcelona and Smith's believing p. If

---

[2] *Op. cit.* Criticisms of Clark's analysis will be discussed below.

Smith had come to believe p by reading a letter from Brown postmarked in Barcelona, then we might say that Smith knew p. Alternatively, if Jones did own a Ford, and his owning the Ford was manifested by his offer of a ride to Smith, and this in turn resulted in Smith's believing p, then we would say that Smith knew p. Thus, one thing that seems to be missing in this example is a causal connection between the fact that makes p true [or simply: the fact that p] and Smith's belief of p. The requirement of such a *causal connection* is what I wish to add to the traditional analysis.

To see that this requirement is satisfied in all cases of (empirical) knowledge, we must examine a variety of such causal connections. Clearly, only a sketch of the important kinds of cases is possible here.

Perhaps the simplest case of a causal chain connecting some fact p with someone's belief of p is that of *perception*. I wish to espouse a version of the causal theory of perception, in essence that defended by H. P. Grice.[3] Suppose that S sees that there is a vase in front of him. How is this to be analyzed? I shall not attempt a complete analysis of this, but a necessary condition of S's seeing that there is a vase in front of him is that there be a certain kind of causal connection between the presence of the vase and S's believing that a vase is present. I shall not attempt to describe this causal process in detail. Indeed, to a large extent, a description of this process must be regarded as a problem for the special sciences, not for philosophy. But a certain causal process—viz., that which standardly takes place when we say that so-and-so *sees* such-and-such—must occur. That our ordinary concept of sight (i.e., knowledge acquired by sight) includes a causal requirement is shown by the fact that if the relevant causal process is absent we would withhold the assertion that so-and-so *saw* such-and-such. Suppose that, although a vase is directly in front of S, a laser photograph[4]

[3] "The Causal Theory of Perception," *Proceedings of the Aristotelian Society*, Supp. Vol. XXXV (1961).

[4] If a laser photograph (hologram) is illuminated by light waves, especially waves from a laser, the effect of the hologram on the viewer

is interposed between it and S, thereby blocking it from S's view. The photograph, however, is one of a vase (a different vase), and when it is illuminated by light waves from a laser, it looks to S exactly like a real vase. When the photograph is illuminated, S forms the belief that there is a vase in front of him. Here we would deny that S *sees* that there is a vase in front of him, for his view of the real vase is completely blocked, so that it has no causal role in the formation of his belief. Of course, S might *know* that there was a vase in front of him even if the photograph is blocking his view. Someone else, in a position to see the vase, might tell S that there is a vase in front of him. Here the presence of the vase might be a causal ancestor of S's belief, but the causal process would not be a (purely) *perceptual* one. S could not be said to *see* that there is a vase in front of him. For this to be true, there must be a causal process, but one of a very special sort, connecting the presence of the vase with S's belief.

I shall here assume that perceptual knowledge of facts is noninferential. This is merely a simplifying procedure, and not essential to my account. Certainly a percipient does not *infer* facts about physical objects from the state of his brain or from the stimulation of his sense organs. He need not know about these goings-on at all. But some epistemologists maintain that we directly perceive only sense data and that we infer physical-object facts from them. This view could be accommodated within my analysis. I could say that physical-object facts cause sense data, that people directly perceive sense data, and that they infer the physical object facts from the sense data. This kind of process would be fully accredited by my analysis, which will allow for knowledge based on inference. But for purposes of exposition it will be convenient to regard perceptual knowledge of external facts as independent of any inference.

---

is exactly as if the object were being seen. It preserves three-dimensionality completely, and even gives appropriate parallax effects as the viewer moves relative to it. Cf. E. N. Leith and J. Upatnieks, "Photography by Laser," *Scientific American*, CCXII, 6 (June 1965): 24.

Here the question arises about the *scope* of perceptual knowledge. By perception I can know noninferentially that there is a vase in front of me. But can I know noninferentially that the painting I am viewing is a Picasso? It is unnecessary to settle such issues here. Whether the knowledge of such facts is to be classed as inferential or noninferential, my analysis can account for it. So the scope of noninferential knowledge may be left indeterminate.

I turn next to memory, i.e., knowledge that is based, in part, on memory. Remembering, like perceiving, must be regarded as a causal process. S remembers p at time t only if S's believing p at an earlier time is a cause of his believing p at t. Of course, not every causal connection between an earlier belief and a later one is a case of remembering. As in the case of perception, however, I shall not try to describe this process in detail. This is a job mainly for the scientist. Instead, the kind of causal process in question is to be identified simply by example, by "pointing" to paradigm cases of remembering. Whenever causal processes are of that kind—whatever that kind is, precisely—they are cases of remembering.[5]

A causal connection between earlier belief (or knowledge) of p and later belief (knowledge) of p is certainly a necessary ingredient in memory.[6] To remember a fact is not simply to believe it at t_0 and also to believe it at t_1. Nor does someone's knowing a fact at t_0 and his knowing it at t_1 entail that he remembers it at t_1. He may have perceived the fact at t_0, forgotten it, and then relearned it at t_1 by someone's telling it to him. Nor does the inclusion of a memory "impression"—a feeling of remembering—ensure that one really remembers.

---

[5] For further defense of this kind of procedure, with attention to perception, cf. Grice, *op. cit.* A detailed causal analysis of remembering is presented by C. B. Martin and Max Deutscher, "Remembering," *The Philosophical Review*, LXXV.2, ns 414 (April 1966): 161–196.

[6] Causal connections can hold between states of affairs, such as believings, as well as between events. If a given event or state, in conjunction with other events or states, "leads to" or "results in" another event or state (or the same state obtaining at a later time), it will be called a "cause" of the latter. I shall also speak of "facts" being causes.

Suppose S perceives p at t_0, but forgets it at t_1. At t_2 he begins to believe p again because someone tells him p, but at t_2 he has no memory impression of p. At t_3 we artificially stimulate in S a memory impression of p. It does not follow that S remembers p at t_3. The description of the case suggests that his believing p at t_0 has no causal effect whatever on his believing p at t_3; and if we accepted this fact, we would deny that he remembers p at t_3.

Knowledge can be acquired by a combination of perception and memory. At t_0, the fact p causes S to believe p, by perception. S's believing p at t_0 results, via memory, in S's believing p at t_1. Thus, the fact p is a cause of S's believing p at t_1, and S can be said to know p at t_1. But not all knowledge results from perception and memory alone. In particular, much knowledge is based on *inference*.

As I shall use the term 'inference,' to say that S knows p by "inference" does not entail that S went through an explicit, conscious process of reasoning. It is not necessary that he have "talked to himself," saying something like "Since such-and-such is true, p must also be true." My belief that there is a fire in the neighborhood is based on, or inferred from, my belief that I hear a fire engine. But I have not gone through a process of explicit reasoning, saying "There's a fire engine; therefore there must be a fire." Perhaps the word 'inference' is ordinarily used only where explicit reasoning occurs; if so, my use of the term will be somewhat broader than its ordinary use.

Suppose S perceives that there is solidified lava in various parts of the countryside. On the basis of this belief, plus various "background" beliefs about the production of lava, S concludes that a nearby mountain erupted many centuries ago. Let us assume that this is a highly warranted inductive inference, one which gives S adequate evidence for believing that the mountain did erupt many centuries ago. Assuming this proposition is true, does S know it? This depends on the nature of the causal process that induced his belief. If there is a continuous causal chain of the sort he envisages connecting the fact that the mountain erupted with his belief of this fact, then S knows it. If there is no such causal chain, however, S does not know that proposition.

Suppose that the mountain erupts, leaving lava around the countryside. The lava remains there until S perceives it and infers that the mountain erupted. Then S does know that the mountain erupted. But now suppose that, after the mountain has erupted, a man somehow removes all the lava. A century later, a different man (not knowing of the real volcano) decides to make it look as if there had been a volcano, and therefore puts lava in appropriate places. Still later, S comes across this lava and concludes that the mountain erupted centuries ago. In this case, S cannot be said to know the proposition. This is because the fact that the mountain did erupt is not a cause of S's believing that it erupted. A necessary condition of S's knowing p is that his believing p be connected with p by a causal chain.

In the first case, where S knows p, the causal connection may be diagrammed as in Figure 1. (p) is the fact that the mountain erupted at such-and-such a time. (q) is the fact that lava is (now) present around the countryside. 'B' stands for a belief, the expression in parentheses indicating the proposition believed, and the subscript designating the believer. (r) is a "background" proposition, describing the ways in which lava is produced and how it solidifies. Solid arrows in the diagram represent causal connections; dotted arrows represent inferences. Notice that, in Figure 1, there is not only an arrow connecting (q) with S's belief of (q), but also an arrow connecting (p) with (q). In the suggested variant of the lava case, the latter arrow would be missing, showing that there is no continuous causal chain connecting (p) with S's belief of (p). Therefore, in that variant case, S could not be said to know (p).

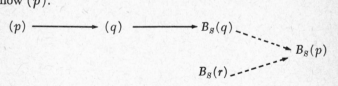

FIGURE 1

I have said that p is causally connected to S's belief of p, in the case diagrammed in Figure 1. This raises the question, however, of whether the inferential part of the chain is itself a causal chain. In other words, is S's belief of q a cause of his believing p? This is a question to which I shall not try to give a definitive answer here. I am inclined to say that inference *is* a causal process, that is, that when someone *bases* his belief of one proposition on his belief of a set of other propositions, then his belief of the latter propositions can be considered a cause of his belief of the former proposition. But I do not wish to rest my thesis on this claim. All I do claim is that, if a chain of inferences is "added" to a causal chain, then the entire chain is causal. In terms of our diagram, a chain consisting of solid arrows plus dotted arrows is to be considered a causal chain, though I shall not take a position on the question of whether the dotted arrows represent causal connections. Thus, in Figure 1, p is a cause of S's belief of p, whether or not we regard S's belief of q a cause of his belief of p.[7]

Consider next a case of knowledge based on "testimony." This too can be analyzed causally. p causes a person T to believe p, by perception. T's belief of p gives rise to (causes) his asserting p. T's asserting p causes S, by auditory perception, to believe that T is asserting p. S infers that T believes p, and from this, in turn, he infers that p is a fact. There is a continuous causal chain from p to S's believing p, and thus, assuming that each of S's inferences is warranted, S can be said to know p.

This causal chain is represented in Figure 2. 'A' refers to an

---

[7] A fact can be a cause of a belief even if it does not *initiate* the belief. Suppose I believe that there is a lake in a certain locale, this belief having started in a manner quite unconnected with the existence of the lake. Continuing to have the belief, I go to the locale and perceive the lake. At this juncture, the existence of the lake becomes a cause of my believing that there is a lake there. This is analogous to a table top that is supported by four legs. When a fifth leg is inserted flush beneath the table top, it too becomes a cause of the table top's not falling. It has a causal role in the support of the table top even though, before it was inserted, the table top was adequately supported.

act of asserting a proposition, the expression in parentheses indicating the proposition asserted and the subscript designating the agent. (q), (r), (u), and (v) are background propositions. (q) and (r), for example, pertain to T's sincerity; they help S conclude, from the fact that T asserted p, that T really believes p.

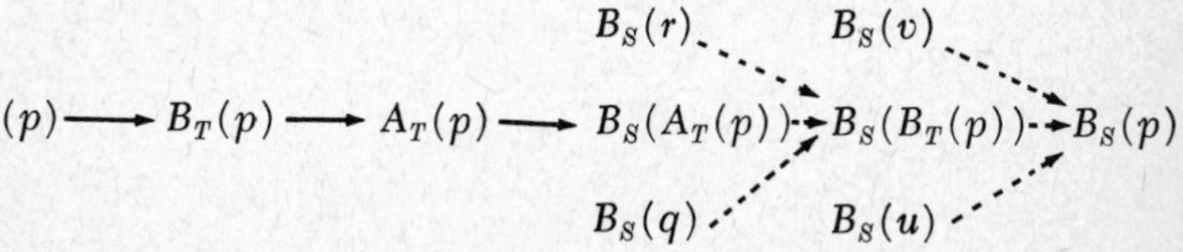

$$(p) \longrightarrow B_T(p) \longrightarrow A_T(p) \longrightarrow B_S(A_T(p)) \dashrightarrow B_S(B_T(p)) \dashrightarrow B_S(p)$$

with $B_S(r)$, $B_S(q)$ feeding into $B_S(B_T(p))$ and $B_S(v)$, $B_S(u)$ feeding into $B_S(p)$.

FIGURE 2

In this case, as in the lava case, S knows p because he has correctly reconstructed the causal chain leading from p to the evidence for p that S perceives, in this case, T's asserting (p). This correct reconstruction is shown in the diagram by S's inference "mirroring" the rest of the causal chain. Such a correct reconstruction is a necessary condition of knowledge based on inference. To see this, consider the following example. A newspaper reporter observes p and reports it to his newspaper. When printed, however, the story contains a typographical error so that it asserts not-p. When reading the paper, however, S fails to see the word 'not', and takes the paper to have asserted p. Trusting the newspaper, he infers that p is true. Here we have a continuous causal chain leading from p to S's believing p; yet S does not know p. S thinks that p resulted in a report to the newspaper about p and that this report resulted in its printing the statement p. Thus, his reconstruction of the causal chain is mistaken. But, if he is to know p, his reconstruction must contain no mistakes. Though he need not reconstruct *every* detail of the causal chain, he must reconstruct all the important links.[8] An additional requirement for knowledge

[8] Clearly we cannot require someone to reconstruct every detail, since this would involve knowledge of minute physical phenomena, for example, of which ordinary people are unaware. On the other hand, it is

based on inference is that the knower's inferences be warranted. That is, the propositions on which he bases his belief of p must genuinely confirm p very highly, whether deductively or inductively. Reconstructing a causal chain merely by lucky guesses does not yield knowledge.

With the help of our diagrams, we can contrast the traditional analysis of knowing with Clark's analysis (*op. cit.*) and contrast each of these with my own analysis. The traditional analysis makes reference to just three features of the diagrams. First, it requires that p be true; i.e., that (p) appear in the diagram. Secondly, it requires that S believe p; i.e., that S's belief of p appear in the diagram. Thirdly, it requires that S's inferences, if any, be warranted; i.e., that the sets of beliefs that are at the tail of a dotted arrow must jointly highly confirm the belief at the head of these arrows. Clark proposes a further requirement for knowledge. He requires that *each* of the beliefs in S's chain of inference be *true*. In other words, whereas the traditional analysis requires a fact to correspond to S's belief of p, Clark requires that a fact correspond to *each* of S's beliefs on which he based his belief of p. Thus, corresponding to each belief on the right side of the diagram there must be a fact on the left side. (My diagrams omit facts corresponding to the "background" beliefs.)

As Clark's analysis stands, it seems to omit an element of the diagrams that my analysis requires, viz., the arrows indicating causal connections. Now Clark might reformulate his analysis so as to make implicit reference to these causal connections. If he required that the knower's beliefs include *causal beliefs* (of the relevant sort), then his requirement that these beliefs be true would amount to the requirement that there *be* causal chains of the sort I require. This interpretation of Clark's analysis would make it almost equivalent to mine, and would enable him to avoid some objections that have been raised against him. But he has not explicitly formulated his analysis this way, and it therefore remains deficient in this respect.

---

difficult to give criteria to identify which details, in general, are "important." This will vary substantially from case to case.

Before turning to the problems facing Clark's analysis, more must be said about my own analysis. So far, my examples may have suggested that, if S knows p, the fact that p is a cause of his belief of p. This would clearly be wrong, however. Let us grant that I can know facts about the future. Then, if we required that the known facts cause the knower's belief, we would have to countenance "backward" causation. My analysis, however, does not face this dilemma. The analysis requires that there be a causal *connection* between p and S's belief, not necessarily that p be a *cause* of S's belief. p and S's belief of p can also be causally connected in a way that yields knowledge if both p and S's belief of p have a *common* cause. This can be illustrated as follows.

T intends to go downtown on Monday. On Sunday, T tells S of his intention. Hearing T say he will go downtown, S infers that T really does intend to go downtown. And from this S concludes that T *will* go downtown on Monday. Now suppose that T fulfills his intention by going downtown on Monday. Can S be said to know that he would go downtown? If we ever can be said to have knowledge of the future, this is a reasonable candidate for it. So let us say S did know that proposition. How can my analysis account for S's knowledge? T's going downtown on Monday clearly cannot be a cause of S's believing, on Sunday, that he would go downtown. But there is a fact that is the *common* cause of T's going downtown and of S's belief that he would go downtown, viz., T's intending (on Sunday) to go downtown. This intention resulted in his going downtown and also resulted in S's believing that he would go downtown. This causal connection between S's belief and the fact believed allows us to say that S *knew* that T would go downtown.

The example is diagrammed in Figure 3. (p) = T's going downtown on Monday. (q) = T's intending (on Sunday) to go downtown on Monday. (r) = T's telling S (on Sunday) that he will go downtown on Monday. (u) and (v) are relevant background propositions pertaining to T's honesty, resoluteness, etc. The diagram reveals that q is a cause both of p and of S's belief of p. Cases of this kind I shall call *Pattern 2*

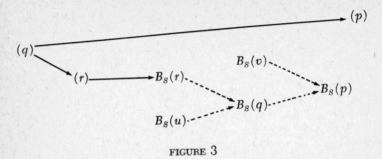

cases of knowledge. Figures 1 and 2 exemplify *Pattern 1* cases of knowledge.

Notice that the causal connection between q and p is an essential part of S's knowing p. Suppose, for example, that T's intending (on Sunday) to go downtown does not result in, or cause, T's going downtown on Monday. Suppose that T, after telling S that he would go downtown, changes his mind. Nevertheless, on Monday he is kidnapped and forced, at the point of a gun, to go downtown. Here both q and p actually occur, but they are not causally related. The diagram in Figure 3 would have to be amended by deleting the arrow connecting (q) with (p). But if the rest of the facts of the original case remain the same, S could not be said to know p. It would be false to say that S knew, on Sunday, that T would go downtown on Monday.

Pattern 2 cases of knowledge are not restricted to knowledge of the future. I know that smoke was coming out of my chimney last night. I know this because I remember perceiving a fire in my fireplace last night, and I infer that the fire caused smoke to rise out of the chimney. This case exemplifies Pattern 2. The smoke's rising out of the chimney is not a causal factor of my belief. But the fact that there was a fire in the fireplace was a cause both of my belief that smoke was coming out of the chimney and of the fact that smoke was coming out of the chimney. If we supplement this case slightly, we can make my knowledge exemplify *both* Pattern 1 and Pattern 2.

Suppose that a friend tells me today that he perceived smoke coming out of my chimney last night and I base my continued belief of this fact on his testimony. Then the fact was a cause of my current belief of it, as well as an *effect* of another fact that caused my belief. In general, numerous and diverse kinds of causal connections can obtain between a given fact and a given person's belief of that fact.

Let us now examine some objections to Clark's analysis and see how the analysis presented here fares against them. John Turk Saunders and Narayan Champawat[9] have raised the following counterexample to Clark's analysis:

> Suppose that Smith believes
> > (p) Jones owns a Ford
> because his friend Brown whom he knows to be generally reliable and honest yesterday told Smith that Jones had always owned a Ford. Brown's information was correct, but today Jones sells his Ford and replaces it with a Volkswagen. An hour later Jones is pleased to find that he is the proud owner of two cars: he has been lucky enough to win a Ford in a raffle. Smith's belief in p is not only justified and true, but is fully grounded, e.g., we suppose that each link in the . . . chain of Smith's grounds is true (p. 8).

Clearly Smith does not know p; yet he seems to satisfy Clark's analysis of knowing.

Smith's lack of knowledge can be accounted for in terms of my analysis. Smith does not know p because his believing p is not causally related to p, Jones's owning a Ford *now*. This can be seen by examining Figure 4. In the diagram, (p) = Jones's owning a Ford now; (q) = Jones's having always owned a Ford (until yesterday); (r) = Jones's winning a Ford in a raffle today. (t), (u), and (v) are background propositions. (v), for example, deals with the likelihood of someone's con-

9 "Mr. Clark's Definition of 'Knowledge'," *Analysis*, XXV.1, ns 103 (October 1964): 8–9.

tinuing to own the same car today that he owned yesterday.
The subscript 'B' designates Brown, and the subscript 'S'
designates Smith. Notice the absence of an arrow connecting
(p) with (q). The absence of this arrow represents the absence of a causal relation between (q) and (p). Jones's owning a Ford in the past (until yesterday) is not a cause of his
owning one now. Had he continued owning the same Ford
today that he owned yesterday, there would be a causal connection between q and p and, therefore, a causal connection
between p and Smith's believing p. This causal connection
would exemplify Pattern 2. But, as it happened, it is purely a
coincidence that Jones owns a Ford today as well as yesterday.
Thus, Smith's belief of p is not connected with p by Pattern 2,
nor is there any Pattern 1 connection between them. Hence,
Smith does not know p.

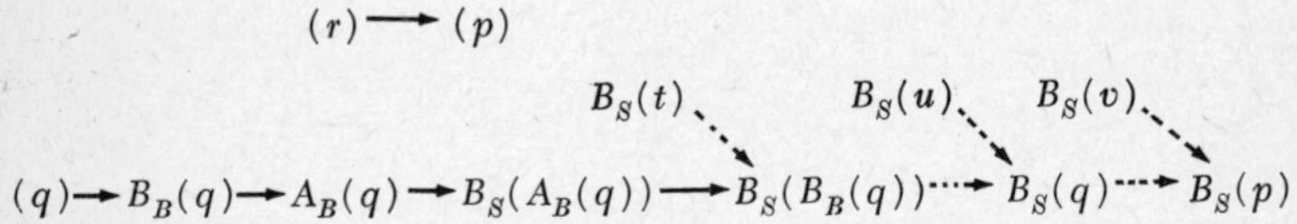

$$(r) \longrightarrow (p)$$

$$B_S(t) \searrow \qquad\qquad B_S(u) \searrow \quad B_S(v) \searrow$$

$$(q) \rightarrow B_B(q) \rightarrow A_B(q) \rightarrow B_S(A_B(q)) \longrightarrow B_S(B_B(q)) \cdots\rightarrow B_S(q) \cdots\rightarrow B_S(p)$$

FIGURE 4

If we supplement Clark's analysis as suggested above, it can
be saved from this counterexample. Though Saunders and
Champawat fail to mention this explicitly, presumably it is one
of Smith's beliefs that Jones's owning a Ford yesterday would
result in Jones's owning a Ford now. This was undoubtedly
one of his grounds for believing that Jones owns a Ford now.
(A complete diagram of S's beliefs relevant to p would include
this belief.) Since this belief is false, however, Clark's analysis
would yield the correct consequence that Smith does not know
p. Unfortunately, Clark himself seems not to have noticed this
point, since Saunders and Champawat's putative counterexample has been allowed to stand.

Another sort of counterexample to Clark's analysis has been
given by Saunders and Champawat and also by Keith Lehrer.

This is a counterexample from which his analysis cannot escape. I shall give Lehrer's example (*op. cit.*) of this sort of difficulty. Suppose Smith bases his belief of

(*p*) Someone in his office owns a Ford

on his belief of four propositions

(*q*) Jones own a Ford.
(*r*) Jones works in his office.
(*s*) Brown owns a Ford.
(*t*) Brown works in his office.

In fact, Smith knows *q*, *r*, and *t*, but he does not know *s* because *s* is false. Since *s* is false, not *all* of Smith's grounds for *p* are true, and, therefore, on Clark's analysis, Smith does not know *p*. Yet clearly Smith does know *p*. Thus, Clark's analysis is *too strong*.

Having seen the importance of a causal chain for knowing, it is fairly obvious how to amend Clark's requirements without making them too weak. We need not require, as Clark does, that *all* of S's grounds be true. What is required is that enough of them be true to ensure the existence of at least *one* causal connection between *p* and S's belief of *p*. In Lehrer's example, Smith thinks that there are two ways in which he knows *p*: via his knowledge of the conjunction of *q* and *r*, and via his knowledge of the conjunction of *s* and *t*. He does not know *p* via the conjunction of *s* and *t*, since *s* is false. But there is a causal connection, via *q* and *r*, between *p* and Smith's belief of *p*. And this connection is enough.

Another sort of case in which one of S's grounds for *p* may be false without preventing him from knowing *p* is where the false proposition is a dispensable background assumption. Suppose S bases his belief of *p* on 17 background assumptions, but only 16 of these are true. If these 16 are strong enough to confirm *p*, then the 17th is dispensable. S can be said to know *p* though one of his grounds is false.

Our discussion of Lehrer's example calls attention to the necessity of a further clarification of the notion of a "causal chain." I said earlier that causal chains with admixtures of inferences are causal chains. Now I wish to add that causal chains with admixtures of logical connections are causal chains. Unless we allow this interpretation, it is hard to see how facts like "Someone in the office owns a Ford" or "All men are mortal" could be *causally* connected with beliefs thereof.

The following principle will be useful: *If x is logically related to y and if y is a cause of z, then x is a cause of z.* Thus, suppose that q causes S's belief of q and that r causes S's belief of r. Next suppose that S infers q & r from his belief of q and of r. Then the facts q and r are causes of S's believing q & r. But the fact q & r is logically related to the fact q and to the fact r. Therefore, using the principle enunciated above, the fact q & r is a cause of S's believing q & r.

In Lehrer's case another logical connection is involved: a connection between an existential fact and an instance thereof. Lehrer's case is diagrammed in Figure 5. In addition to the usual conventions, logical relationships are represented by double solid lines. As the diagram shows, the fact p—someone in Smith's office owning a Ford—is logically related to the fact q & r—Jones's owning a Ford and Jones's working in Smith's office. The fact q & r is, in turn, logically related to the fact q and to the fact r. q causes S's belief of q and, by inference, his belief of q & r and of p. Similarly, r is a cause of S's belief of p. Hence, by the above principle, p is a cause of S's belief of p. Since Smith's inferences are warranted, even setting aside his belief of s & t, he knows p.

In a similar way, universal facts may be causes of beliefs thereof. The fact that all men are mortal is logically related to its instances: John's being mortal, George's being mortal, Oscar's being mortal, etc. Now suppose that S perceives George, John, Oscar, etc., to be mortal (by seeing them die). He infers from these facts that all men are mortal, an inference which, I assume, is warranted. Since each of the facts, John is mortal, George is mortal, Oscar is mortal, etc., is a cause of S's believing that fact, each is also a cause of S's believing that

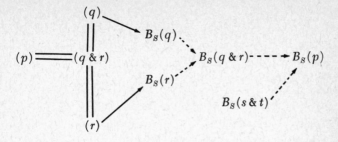

all men are mortal. Moreover, since the universal fact that all men are mortal is logically related to each of these particular facts, this universal fact is a cause of S's belief of it. Hence, S can be said to know that all men are mortal. In analogous fashions, S can know various other logically compound propositions.

We can now formulate the analysis of knowing as follows:

S knows that p if and only if:
The fact p is causally connected in an "appropriate" way with S's believing p.

"Appropriate," knowledge-producing causal processes include the following:

(1) perception
(2) memory
(3) a causal chain, exemplifying either Pattern 1 or 2, which is correctly reconstructed by inferences, each of which is warranted. (Background propositions help warrant an inference only if they are true.)[10]
(4) combinations of (1), (2), and (3)

---

[10] Perhaps background propositions that help warrant S's inference must be *known* by S, as well as true. This requirement could be added without making our analysis of "S knows that *p*" circular. For these propositions would not include *p*. In other words, the analysis of knowledge could be regarded as recursive.

We have seen that this analysis is *stronger* than the traditional analysis in certain respects: the causal requirement and
the correct-reconstruction requirement are absent from the
older analysis. These additional requirements enable my
analysis to circumvent Gettier's counterexamples to the traditional one. But my analysis is *weaker* than the traditional
analysis in another respect. In at least one popular interpretation of the traditional analysis, a knower must be able to justify
or give evidence for any proposition he knows. For S to know
p at t, S must be able, at t, to *state* his justification for believing p, or his grounds for p. My analysis makes no such requirement, and the absence of this requirement enables me to
account for cases of knowledge that would wrongly be excluded by the traditional analysis.

I know now, for example, that Abraham Lincoln was born in
1809.[11] I originally came to know this fact, let us suppose, by
reading an encyclopedia article. I believed that this encyclopedia was trustworthy and that its saying Lincoln was born in
1809 must have resulted from the fact that Lincoln was indeed
born in 1809. Thus, my original knowledge of this fact was
founded on a warranted inference. But now I no longer remember this inference. I remember that Lincoln was born in 1809,
but not that this is stated in a certain encyclopedia. I no longer
have any pertinent beliefs that highly confirm the proposition
that Lincoln was born in 1809. Nevertheless, I know this proposition now. My original knowledge of it was preserved until
now by the causal process of memory.

Defenders of the traditional analysis would doubtlessly deny
that I really do know Lincoln's birth year. This denial, however, stems from a desire to protect their analysis. It seems
clear that many things we know were originally learned in a
way that we no longer remember. The range of our knowledge
would be drastically reduced if these items were denied the
status of knowledge.

Other species of knowledge without explicit evidence could

[11] This kind of case is drawn from an unpublished manuscript of
Gilbert Harman.

also be admitted by my analysis. Notice that I have not closed the list of "appropriate" causal processes. Leaving the list open is desirable, because there may be some presently controversial causal processes that we may later deem "appropriate" and, therefore, knowledge-producing. Many people now doubt the legitimacy of claims to extrasensory perception. But if conclusive evidence were to establish the existence of causal processes connecting physical facts with certain persons' beliefs without the help of standard perceptual processes, we might decide to call such beliefs items of knowledge. This would be another species of knowledge in which the knower might be unable to justify or defend his belief. My analysis allows for the possibility of such knowledge, though it doesn't commit one to it.

Special comments are in order about knowledge of our own mental states. This is a very difficult and controversial topic, so I hesitate to discuss it, but something must be said about it. Probably there are some mental states that are clearly distinct from the subject's beliefs that he is in such a state. If so, then there is presumably a causal process connecting the existence of such states with the subject's belief thereof. We may add this kind of process to the list of "appropriate" causal processes. The more difficult cases are those in which the state is hardly distinguishable from the subject's believing that he is in that state. My being in pain and my believing that I am in pain are hardly distinct states of affairs. If there is no distinction here between the believing and the believed, how can there be a causal connection between them? For the purposes of the present analysis, we may regard identity as a "limiting" or "degenerate" case of a causal connection, just as zero may be regarded as a "limiting" or "degenerate" case of a number. It is not surprising that knowledge of one's own mental state should turn out to be a limiting or degenerate case of knowledge. Philosophers have long recognized its peculiar status. While some philosophers have regarded it as a paradigm case of knowledge, others have claimed that we have no "knowledge" of our mental states at all. A theory of knowledge that makes knowledge of one's own mental states rather different from garden-variety species of knowledge is, in so far forth, acceptable and even welcome.

In conclusion, let me answer some possible objections to my analysis. It might be doubted whether a causal analysis adequately provides the meaning of the word 'knows' or of the sentence (-schema) "S knows p." But I am not interested in giving the *meaning* of "S knows p"; only its *truth conditions*. I claim to have given one correct set of truth conditions for "S knows p." Truth conditions of a sentence do not always provide its meaning. Consider, for example, the following truth-conditions statement: "The sentence 'Team T wins the baseball game' is true if and only if team T has more runs at the end of the game than the opposing team." This statement fails to provide the meaning of the sentence 'Team T wins the baseball game'; for it fails to indicate an essential part of the meaning of that sentence, viz., that to win a game is to achieve the presumed goal of playing it. Someone might fully understand the truth conditions given above and yet fail to understand the meaning of the sentence because he has no understanding of the notion of "winning" in general.

Truth conditions should not be confused with verification conditions. My analysis of "S knows p" does not purport to give procedures for *finding out* whether a person (including oneself) knows a given proposition. No doubt, we sometimes do know that people know certain propositions, for we sometimes know that their beliefs are causally connected (in appropriate ways) with the facts believed. On the other hand, it may often be difficult or even impossible to find out whether this condition holds for a given proposition and a given person. For example, it may be difficult for me to find out whether I really do remember a certain fact that I seem to remember. The difficulties that exist for *finding out* whether someone knows a given proposition do not constitute difficulties for my analysis, however.

In the same vein it should be noted that I have made no attempt to answer skeptical problems. My analysis gives no answer to the skeptic who asks that I start from the content of my own experience and then prove that I know there is a material world, a past, etc. I do not take this to be one of the jobs of giving truth conditions for "S knows that p."

The analysis presented here flies in the face of a well-established tradition in epistemology, the view that epistemological questions are questions of logic or justification, not causal or genetic questions. This traditional view, however, must not go unquestioned. Indeed, I think my analysis shows that the question of whether someone knows a certain proposition is, in part, a causal question, although, of course, the question of what the correct analysis is of "S knows that p" is not a causal question.

Brian Skyrms

The Explication of 'X Knows That *p*'

Edmund Gettier's striking counterexamples to the customary conception of knowledge as justified true belief[1] have brought forth a flurry of discussion on the subject.[2] Several revised definitions have been put forward, and counterexamples to the traditional and revised definitions have proliferated. I believe that all the revised definitions that have appeared are inadequate and that their inadequacy stems from a failure to appreciate the full force of the problems besetting the analysis of knowledge. I shall attempt to exhibit these problems in

From *The Journal of Philosophy*, 64, 12 (June 22, 1967), 373–389. Reprinted by permission of the author and *The Journal of Philosophy*.

[1] Edmund Gettier, "Is Justified True Belief Knowledge?" *Analysis*, XXIII.6, ns 96 (June 1963): 121–123. [Pp. 35–38 of the present volume. Ed.]

[2] Michael Clark, "Knowledge and Grounds: A Comment on Gettier's Paper," *Analysis*, XXIV.2, ns 98 (December 1963): 46–48; Ernest Sosa, "The Analysis of 'Knowledge That P,'" *Analysis*, xxv.2, ns 103 (October 1964): 1–8; John Turk Saunders and Narayan Champawat, "Mr. Clark's Definition of 'Knowledge,'" *Analysis*, xxv.1, ns 103 (October 1964): 8–9; Keith Lehrer, "Knowledge, Truth and Evidence," *Analysis*, xxv.5, ns 105 (April 1965): 168–175 [Pp. 55–66 of the present volume. Ed.] Alvin I. Goldman, "A Causal Theory of Knowing," *The Journal of Philosophy*, LXIV, 12 (June 22, 1967): 357–372. [Pp. 67–87 of the present volume. Ed.] I wish to thank Professors Champawat, Saunders, Sosa, and Goldman for the privilege of reading and discussing their papers with them prior to publication.

their full force, and take some constructive steps toward their solution.

The Traditional Definition of Knowledge. Ever since Plato it has been clear that some cases of true belief are lucky guesses rather than knowledge. It would seem that the relevant distinction can be drawn nicely by defining knowledge as justified true belief. 'Justified' is, of course, a notoriously ambiguous word; but it is clear that the justification here intended is epistemological rather than legal or moral. Since epistemological justification is usually taken to be a matter of good evidence, the following recommends itself as a more explicit rendering of the traditional definition of knowledge:

X knows that p iff there is a body of evidence 'e'[3] such that:

(1) X possesses 'e'
(2) 'e' is good evidence for 'p'
(3) X believes that p on the basis of (1) and (2)[4]
(4) 'p' is true

Ignoring, for the moment, any counterexamples, this definition is immediately suspect of circularity. "X possesses 'e'" appears

[3] The distinction between quoted sentences and "that"-ed sentences is important and raises questions relevant to the analysis of "X knows that p." In this paper, I choose to ignore these questions in order to concentrate on others. Furthermore, in order to avoid awkward locutions I shall not strictly observe this distinction. One way of achieving uniformity would be to read the quotes throughout as Sellars' dot quotes (see Wilfrid Sellars, "Abstract Entities," *Review of Metaphysics,* xvi, 4 (1963): 627–671). I will impose on the reader's good will by asking him to read in uniformity in whichever way is consistent with his philosophical position on these issues, and to verify that this matter in no way affects the main conclusions of this paper.

[4] This statement of qualification 3 is superior to the simpler statement, "X believes that p." The human mind is often a disorderly thing, and it is possible for X to be in possession of both good evidence for 'p' and bad evidence for 'p'; fail to make the connection between the good evidence and 'p'; and believe 'p' on the basis of the bad evidence. If 'p' turns out to be true, we should call this a lucky guess rather than a case of knowledge.

to be a transparent disguise for "X knows that e." Such circularity could be rendered innocuous if the foregoing could be construed as the inductive clause in a definition of knowledge of the form:

X knows that p iff either the conditions of (A) or the conditions of (B) are satisfied:

(A) Conditions for Basic Knowledge:
    (1) 'p' R X
    (2) X believes that p, and his belief is not based on evidence
    (3) 'p' is true
(B) Conditions for Non-Basic Knowledge: there is some body of evidence 'e' such that:
    (1) X knows that e
    (2) 'e' is good evidence for 'p'[5]
    (3) X believes that p on the basis of (1) and (2)
    (4) 'p' is true

However, it is by no means clear that there is an appropriate relation R that defines a class of basic statements for each person such that the conditions of (A) formulate a sufficient condition for knowledge *and* the entire definition formulates a *necessary* and sufficient condition for knowledge.[6] (Nor is it

---

[5] Since we no longer run the risk of vicious circularity in requiring that X have a certain type of knowledge (other than knowledge that p) in the conditions of (B), we might wish to replace condition (2) with (2'): X knows that 'e' is good evidence for 'p'; and to replace (3) with (3'): X believes that p on the basis of the knowledge referred to in (1) and (2'). Such a revision would be motivated by the following concern. It is possible that 'e' is good evidence for 'p' and that X believes that 'e' is good evidence for 'p', but that X has arrived at this belief through incorrect reasoning (e.g., in a complicated case of statistical inference). In such a case, a tinge of the lucky guess lingers in X's belief that p.

[6] The claim that there is a (nontrivial) relation R such that (A) formulates a sufficient condition for knowledge is a much more modest claim than traditional claims about the existence of a "given." (i) Such a claim does not entail that basic statements are incorrigible (i.e., that 'p' R X & X believes that p logically implies 'p' is true). (ii) Such a

clear that if there is such a relation there is only one.) And among philosophers who hold that there is such a relation and only one, there is no general agreement as to what it is.

The issue of basic knowledge is the Pandora's box of epistemology. It shall remain closed during this discussion, for significant questions about the adequacy of (B) can be asked without becoming enmeshed in questions about the existence or nature of basic knowledge. Let us approach the question of adequacy from a new perspective by shifting our attention from the problem of giving a *definition* of knowledge to the problem of codifying the *rules of rational dialectic*[7] for knowledge claims.

Suppose that Y maintains that X knows that p and that Z is interested in challenging this assertion. Implicit in our conception of knowledge are rules that determine which challenges to a knowledge claim are relevant and which responses are adequate. For example, "But does X really believe that p?" is a relevant challenge to "X knows that p," although "Is X really 7 feet tall?" is not a relevant challenge to "X knows that there is no greatest number." And simply repeating a challenged

claim does not entail that basic statements can be known *only* noninferentially (i.e., that 'p' R X & X knows that p logically implies X has *basic* knowledge that p).

But the *additional* claim that basic knowledge, as defined by (A), is comprehensive enough to account for *all* knowledge via (B) (i.e., that (A) & (B) jointly formulate a *necessary* condition for knowledge) is not so modest. And it becomes less modest with every strengthening of the conditions of (B) (e.g., the revision of (B) proposed in fn. 5). Since the paradoxes to be dealt with in this paper all show that (B) fails to formulate a *sufficient* condition for knowledge, their resolution requires a strengthening of the conditions of (B), and thus a probable decrease in the plausibility of the claim that (A) and (B) jointly formulate a necessary condition for knowledge.

[7] These rules of rational dialectic are to be thought of as part of the pure pragmatics of an ideal language game which is an explication of our natural language game. The relevant sense of pure pragmatics is introduced in section III of my paper: "Nomological Necessity and the Paradoxes of Confirmation," *Philosophy of Science*, XXXIII, 3 (September 1966): 230–249.

statement is never an adequate response to a relevant challenge.

Let us say that Y gives a *completely adequate* response to a challenge by Z if and only if Z can rechallenge only by challenging some part of Y's response. For example, if Z challenges: "Does X really know that p?" and Y responds "Yes, for X believes that p and 'p' is true," then Y has not given a completely adequate response, since Z can rechallenge without calling X's belief or the truth of 'p' into question.

The following is a sample initial segment of a rational dialogue in which Y gives completely adequate responses (where the question mark is to be read as "But is it really the case that . . ."):

Y	Z
X knows that p	? X knows that p
Yes, for q & r & s	? q
Yes, for t & u & v	? u[8]

Let us call a claim of the form: "X knows that p" a *K-claim,* and a challenge to this sort of claim a *K-challenge.* Then some completely adequate responses to K-challenges contain K-claims (although different claims than the claim being defended). If there is basic knowledge, then some completely adequate responses to K-challenges will contain no K-claims. Let us divide the class of all completely adequate responses to a given K-challenge into two subclasses:

S_1: The class of all completely adequate responses that make no K-claim

S_2: The class of all completely adequate responses that make at least one K-claim

---

[8] This is a particularly simple rational dialogue in that Z makes only one challenge at each level. If Z makes multiple challenges, the dialogue can *branch,* with Y giving a response to each challenge and with each of these responses being in turn challenged. Thus, in a sense, the *logical form* of a rational dialogue is that of a *tree* rather than simply a sequence.

without committing ourselves as to whether S_1 is empty or not. We shall say that a set of conditions (on X and 'p') is *dialectically adequate* for basic knowledge if and only if for, any K-challenge,

(DA) A (consistent) claim entails that these conditions are met if and only if it is in S_1

Similarly, for nonbasic knowledge (substituting 'S_2' for 'S_1' in DA). A set of conditions dialectically adequate for basic knowledge together with a set of conditions dialectically adequate for nonbasic knowledge will be said to constitute *adequate rules of rational dialectic* for knowledge.[9] If there is no basic knowledge, then a set of conditions is dialectically adequate for basic knowledge if and only if it is inconsistent.

We can now exhibit some of the advantages of attacking this problem in terms of rules of rational dialectic. The requirements for rules of rational dialectic are weaker than those for definitions. Two sets of conditions can constitute adequate rules of rational dialectic even if they do not constitute an adequate inductive definition. This can occur when the basic knowledge defined by the first set of conditions is not comprehensive enough to account for all knowledge via the inductive clause. The situation in which there is no basic knowledge is a limiting case. Furthermore, if the two sets of conditions are regarded as an inductive definition, we cannot evaluate the adequacy of the sets separately. The question of adequacy for

[9] A full treatment of knowledge along the lines here suggested would require a much more comprehensive and sophisticated theory of rational dialectic than I have at hand. The informal and incomplete machinery I have introduced will suffice to develop the points I wish to make in this paper, and these will, I hope, demonstrate the desirability of further investigation in this field.

When I speak of "adequate rules of rational dialectic for knowledge" I do not intend the word 'adequate' to suggest that these rules suffice, in themselves, to settle *all* questions about the structure of rational dialogues generated by K claims. "Adequate rules of rational dialectic for knowledge," as defined here, are only part of the picture, although they are an *essential* part.

an inductive definition is simply: "Does it generate all cases of knowledge and only cases of knowledge?" We could investigate the adequacy of (B) only qua induction clause for a certain basic clause (A). Pandora's box would have to be opened. From the dialectical standpoint, however, we can give a clear meaning to the question of the adequacy of (B) alone: "Does (B) formulate conditions that are dialectically adequate for nonbasic knowledge?" It is this question that will be examined in the remainder of this paper.

The Gettier Counterexamples: Within the framework of the preceding discussion, Gettier's counterexamples are to be interpreted as showing that (B) is not dialectically adequate for nonbasic knowledge, since (B) fails to satisfy (DA). The following conditions specify a class of Gettier-type counterexamples:

(i) X knows that e

(ii) X knows that 'e' is good evidence for 'o'

(iii) X knows that 'o' entails 'p'

(iv) X knows that 'e' is good evidence of 'p' by virtue of (ii) and (iii)

(v) X believes that p on the basis of the knowledge referred to in (i) and (iv)

(vi) 'p' is true

(vii) 'o' is false

It is clear—or at least becomes clear when we put illustrative flesh on this logical skeleton[10]—that, in this sort of case, X does not really know that p. Now, (i), (iv), (v), and (vi) together entail that the conditions of (B) are met (and indeed that the

[10] Gettier gives two concrete examples, *op. cit.*, pp. 122–123. [Pp. 36–38 of the present volume. Ed.]

Case I is an instance of the general form of Gettier-type counterexamples, with 'o' being 'Ga & $a = (\imath x)(Fx)$' and 'p' being '$G(\imath x)(Fx)$'. 'o' is false since $a \neq (\imath x)(Fx)$, but 'p' is true since $b = (\imath x)(Fx)$ & Gb. Case II is an instance of the general form of Gettier-type counterexamples with 'p' being '$o \lor q$'.

stronger conditions of footnote 4 are met). But if these are given as a response to the challenge '? X knows that p', then there must be relevant rechallenges that do not call any of these into question. Thus (i) and (iv) and (v) and (vi) cannot be a completely adequate response, and (B) fails to satisfy (DA).

It is important to realize that Gettier-type counterexamples are ubiquitous and that the difficulties they raise are genuine. Such counterexamples affect knowledge of both physically necessary and logically necessary statements, as well as contingent statements. As an example of the first case, suppose that a scientist has good evidence for a very general law (or theory represented as a conjunction of laws) T; that T entails a more specific law L; that the scientist, having made the appropriate derivation, knows that the entailment holds and by virtue of this fact knows that the evidence in question is good evidence for L; that he believes L on this basis; that the evidence in question is not direct evidence for L; that L is true and T is false. As an example of the second case, suppose that X is investigating a certain calculus C; that X has good evidence for the assertion that a certain formula F is derivable in C; that this evidence does not consist in his having proved that F is derivable in C (say that he has seen F listed as a thesis of C on page 437 of a book, *The Calculus C,* by an eminent logician; that no one has ever discovered a mistake in the published works of this logician; that he has read several careful reviews of this book which in no way challenge the claim that F is a thesis of C; etc.); that X knows that 'F is derivable in C' entails 'G is derivable in C' by virtue of having constructed a derivation of G from F in C; that he believes that G is derivable in C on this basis; that G is indeed derivable in C but F isn't. Now the statement, 'G is derivable *in* C' is a logically necessary statement for which X has evidentially warranted true belief but not knowledge.

The force of the counterexamples canot simply be explained away. For instance, it will not do simply to regard the counterexamples as demonstrating the inadequacy of truth-functional logic, for (i) Gettier-type counterexamples may be formulated

exclusively in ordinary language and retain their full force, and
(ii) whatever one's position on the "adequacy" of truth-
functional logic it is undisputable that we understand it, that
we can use it in formulating factual claims, and that such
factual claims must be viewed as candidates for knowledge.
Nor can one simply regard the special-consequence condition
(If 'e' is good evidence for 'p' and 'p' entails 'q' then 'e' is good
evidence for 'q')[11] as the sole guilty party, for (i) the special-
consequence condition is eminently plausible on its face, (ii)
it is difficult to see how a formal treatment of the evidential
relation via the probability calculus could do without it, and
(iii) even if the special-consequence condition does not hold
universally, it seems clear that it holds in *at least some* Gettier-
type counterexamples. Thus, the counterexamples are genuine
and must be taken seriously.

Let us focus our attention, for the moment, on a subspecies

[11] If we agree that the special-consequence condition holds uncondi-
tionally, then it provides a powerful new argument for favoring the revision of (B) suggested in footnote 4. Consider K-claims of the form
'X knows that N', where 'N' is a logically necessary statement. Then:

   (i) By the special-consequence condition, any contingent statement
       'p' is good evidence for 'N', for any contingent statement is
       good evidence for some statement, and every statement en-
       tails 'N'.
  (ii) But it does *not* follow that from " 'N' is necessary & X knows
       what we have said in (i)" we may infer "X knows that 'p' is
       good evidence for 'N'." In order to draw the required conclu-
       sion, we need the stronger premise: "X *knows* that 'N' is neces-
       sary" (and perhaps some others).
 (iii) So, where 'p' is necessary, condition B-2 is trivially satisfied,
       whereas condition B-2' is not!
  (iv) It might be argued that, in cases where B-2 is *trivially* satisfied,
       B-3 is not satisfied. But on what a given person bases his be-
       liefs is a contingent psychological matter. Thus the logical
       possibility of circumstances where (B) would fail and the re-
       vision proposed in footnote 4 would succeed must be granted.
       This is sufficient to establish the point at issue, for we are in-
       terested in a *logical analysis* of knowledge, and so examples
       cannot be ruled out of court simply on the grounds that they
       are psychologically bizarre.

of this type of counterexample where 'p' is of the form '$o \vee q$'. This seems to be a likely starting point, for questions about knowledge of disjunctions have a long history of generating philosophical perplexities. It may then be well to begin by asking the basic question: "How is knowledge of disjunctions possible?"

It is clear that knowledge of a disjunction is possible when it is parasitic on knowledge of the disjuncts. Let us call this sort of knowledge of a disjunction *derivative* knowledge. More precisely:

X has derivative knowledge of a disjunction '$p \vee q$' if and only if either (i) or (ii) is satisfied:

  (i) X knows that p and believes that $p \vee q$ on this basis
  (ii) X knows that q and believes that $p \vee q$ on this basis[12, 13]

It is also clear that *nonderivative* knowledge of disjunctions is possible.[14] X may know that he will go to a bar or go home

[12] In the interests of simplicity at this stage of the game, I am leaving unstated the tacit assumption that X knows that a disjunction follows from either of the disjuncts.

[13] The time has come to be a little more explicit about the meaning of the phrase 'on this basis'. We shall use the phrase in such a way that the following three statements will be compatible: "X believes 'p' on the basis of 'q'"; "X believes 'p' on the basis of 'r'"; "X believes 'p' on the basis of 'q & r'." For X to believe 'p' on the basis of 'q' it is not necessary that 'q' be his *sole* ground for believing 'p'. But it is necessary that 'q' alone *would be* sufficient for his belief. Thus, if X believes 'p' on the basis of 'q & r' but even if he had had no beliefs regarding 'r' and retained his belief in 'q', he would still have believed 'p', then X also believes 'p' on the basis of 'q'. On the other hand, it does not follow that, if X believes 'p' on the basis of 'q' and X believes 'r', then X believes 'p' on the basis of 'q & r'. X believes 'p' on the basis of 'q & r' only if both 'q' and 'r' are relevant to his belief that p.

[14] It may perhaps be worth mentioning that there is a connection between the assumption that *all* knowledge of disjunctions is derivative, and the intuitionist propositional calculus. If this assumption, together with some others (notably about negation), is built into rules of rational dialectic, then a claim 'X knows that α' will be ultimately unchallengeable (in a strong sense) only if 'α' is an intuitionist tautology. (This

after the lecture without knowing which he will do. X may know that there will be a sea battle tomorrow or there will not, without knowing whether there will be a sea battle or not. How is such knowledge possible? The obvious answer to this question is that the possibility of nonderivative knowledge rests on the possibility of nonderivative evidentially warranted belief. That is, it is possible to have good evidence for '$p \lor q$' and to believe '$p \lor q$' on this basis, without having evidentially warranted belief in either 'p' or 'q'. Let us then say that:

X has nonderivative knowledge of a disjunction '$p \lor q$' if and only if there is a body of evidence 'e' such that:

  (i) X knows that e
 (ii) X knows that 'e' is good evidence for '$p \lor q$'
(iii) X believes that $p \lor q$ on the basis of the knowledge referred to in (i) and (ii)
 (iv) '$p \lor q$' is true
  (v) It is not the case that (ii) and (iii) hold good with 'p' substituted for '$p \lor q$'. Neither is it the case that (ii) and (iii) hold good with 'q' substituted for '$p \lor q$'

Then X has knowledge of a disjunction if and only if he has either derivative knowledge or nonderivative knowledge of it. But now the counterexamples are blocked! For the Gettier-type counterexamples all are cases where there is no derivative knowledge, but where the evidentially warranted belief is derivative. The requirement that nonderivative knowledge be based on nonderivative evidentially warranted belief does the job. Furthermore, the requirement has an independent rationale. It can be viewed as a *relevance* requirement comparable to other relevance requirements already built into (B). Knowledge requires truth, belief, and evidential warrant; but, in addition, it requires that the three be *connected*. The phrase 'evidentially warranted belief' rather than 'evidential warrant

result can be got by an adaptation of results of Beth and Lorenzen.) A discussion of this interesting connection is, however, beyond the scope of this paper.

and belief' and the phrase 'on the basis of (1) and (2)' in (B-3) formulate the requirements that evidential warrant and belief must be connected. If X believes 'p' (but has no evidence for 'p') and on this basis believes '$p \vee q$'; if X has good evidence for 'q' (but does not believe 'q') and thus has good evidence for '$p \vee q$'; and if '$p \vee q$' is true; we shall deny that X knows that $p \vee q$. By parity of reasoning, we deny that there is knowledge when the evidentially warranted belief flows from one disjunct and the truth from the other. Thus, the requirement that nonderivative knowledge be based on nonderivative evidence is not merely an ad hoc expedient for evading the counterexamples, but rather a natural extension of received relevance requirements for knowledge.

The concepts of derivative and nonderivative knowledge can be generalized[15] as follows:

Derivative Knowledge: X has derivative knowledge that p if and only if there is a statement[16] 'e' such that:

  (i) X knows that e
 (ii) X knows that 'e' entails 'p'
(iii) X believes that p on the basis of the knowledge referred to in (i) and (ii)

---

[15] Actually, I here adopt a slightly different meaning of "derivative" and "nonderivative" knowledge. For example, on the new definition one can have derivative knowledge of '$p \vee \sim p$' without either knowing 'p' or knowing '$\sim p$'. On the new definition one could have derivative knowledge of '$(p \& q) \vee (p \& \sim q)$' based on knowledge of 'p', but, on the old one, derivative knowledge of the first formula would have to be based on knowledge of '$p \& q$' or knowledge of '$p \& \sim q$'. For the duration of this paper I always intend the terms to be taken in their new sense. It is, however, the old sense that is relevant to intuitionist logic.

[16] It is time to resolve the ambiguity in 'body of evidence'. The phrase could be meant to be taken as referring to a set of statements, or to a statement (which might be of the form of a long conjunction). The second alternative is here adopted. For an immediate reason, it will suffice to note that under the first alternative (i) would not make sense. However, that difficulty could be taken care of by a rephrasing of (i). More decisive reasons will emerge as the discussion proceeds.

Nonderivative Knowledge: X has nonderivative knowledge that p if and only if there is a statement 'e' such that:

(i) X knows that e
(ii) X knows that 'e' is good evidence for 'p'
(iii) X believes that p on the basis of the knowledge referred to in (i) and (ii)
(iv) 'p' is true
(v) There is no statement 'q' (other than 'p') such that:
   (a) X knows that 'e' is good evidence for 'q'
   (b) X knows that 'q' entails 'p'
   (c) X believes that 'p' on the basis of the knowledge referred to in (a) and (b)

We can now say that, in general, X has (nonbasic) knowledge that p if and only if X has derivative knowledge that p or X has nonderivative knowledge that p; and the Gettier-type counterexamples are blocked. Transposing these results into the context of rules of rational dialectic for knowledge, we can say that, when Y makes a K-claim, Z should first query: "Basic or Nonbasic Knowledge?" If the answer is "Nonbasic," then Z should query: "Derivative or Nonderivative Knowledge?" From then on, the foregoing conditions establish the rules of rational dialectic for nonderivative knowledge.

The Causal Counterexamples:[17] A significant part of our knowledge is of the type based on signs, symptoms, and indicators.[18] Let us call such knowledge *knowledge of type C,*

---

[17] This section contains examples that show the inadequacies of the revised definitions of knowledge put forward by Clark, Sosa, Lehrer, and Goldman in the articles mentioned in footnote 2. In particular, the barometer and pyromaniac examples are counterexamples to the definitions of Clark, Sosa, Lehrer; the example of the man whose head has been cut off serves as a counterexample to Goldman's causal analysis of knowledge.

[18] It is clear that our knowledge of laws of nature is not of this type, but it is an open question how much of our other knowledge is of this type. There are strong arguments to the effect that a great deal of our other knowledge is of this type. See Hume's discussion in section IV of

without claiming to have precisely delimited its scope. Some knowledge of type C is derivative knowledge. When X knows the appropriate covering law, knows the initial conditions, makes the requisite deductions, and bases his belief on the foregoing, then he may have derivative knowledge. But clearly not all knowledge of type C is derivative knowledge. But when we turn our attention to nonderivative knowledge of type C, we are confronted with a new class of counterexamples which are not blocked by the latest set of conditions. Here are two of them:

Example 1: Consider a society that knows how to construct barometers but is ignorant of the meteorological theories relevant to their uses. Suppose, however, that it has been observed that falling barometers have always been a reliable preindicator of impending rain. And suppose that an individual X observes a barometer falling and thus believes that it will rain, and that it does, in fact, rain. Then his belief is true, and, by the usual canons of evidence, justified. But suppose further that *in this case* the barometer did not fall because of falling air pressure, but because the internal mechanism went haywire. Thus there was no causal relation, *in this instance*, between the action of the barometer and the impending rain, although we shall assume that in the previous observed instances which established barometers as reliable preindicators, the barometers were in good condition, and there was an underlying causal connection. I assume that we would all agree that X did not *know* that it was going to rain. In this instance, he was just lucky.

Example 2: A pyromaniac has just purchased a box of Sure-Fire Matches. He has done so many times before, and has noted that they have always lit when struck unless they were wet. Furthermore, he has a certain rudimentary knowledge of chemistry—enough for him to know that oxygen must be present for things to burn and enough to assure him that the ob-

An *Inquiry Concerning Human Understanding* and Grünbaum's discussion of pre- and post-indicator states in "Temporally-asymmetric Principles, Parity between Explanation and Prediction, and Mechanism versus Teleology," *Philosophy of Science,* xxix, 2 (April 1962): 146–170.

served regularity between matches' being struck and their lighting is not merely a spurious correlation. He ascertains that the matches are dry and that there is plenty of oxygen present. He now proceeds to strike the match, confident in the belief that it will light. It does. Again, we have a case of a justified true belief. But let us assume that unbeknownst to our friend, certain impurities got into this match at the factory which raised its combustion temperature above the temperature that could be attained by friction when it is struck. Assume further that an extremely rare burst of Q-radiation happened to arrive at the very time and place the match was being struck, igniting it, and enabling our friend to accomplish his purpose. It is clear that he did not *know* that the match would strike.

The basic animating principles of these examples appear to be as follows: Let '$p \rightarrow q$' abbreviate " 'p' is a causally sufficient condition for 'q'."[19] Now if 'e' is a body of evidence which is good evidence for '$(x)(Fx \rightarrow Gx)$', it would seem that we must grant that 'e & Fa' is good evidence for 'Ga'.[20] Since we do not require good evidence to guarantee the truth of that for which it is evidence, it is possible that 'e' is true, that 'e' is good evidence for '$(x)(Fx \rightarrow Gx)$' and yet that $(\exists x) \sim (Fx \rightarrow Gx)$.[21]

[19] The meaning of my symbolism can be rendered more precise as follows:
  (i) Call that subset of the class of all possible state descriptions whose members are just those state descriptions in which the laws of nature hold, *the set of all physically possible state descriptions.*
  (ii) '$p \rightarrow q$' is true if and only if 'q' holds in all physically possible state descriptions in which 'p' holds.
  (iii) A universally quantified formula is true if and only if all its substitution instances are true.

[20] See Carnap's discussion of the instance confirmation of a law in *Logical Foundations of Probability*, 2nd ed. (Chicago: University Press, 1962), pp. 571–575.

[21] This can occur even if we have a great deal of background knowledge ruling out the possibility that 'e' represents a totally accidental correlation; for instance, in cases where, in fact: $(x)[(Fx$ & $F'x) \rightarrow Gx]$ but $(x) \sim (Fx \rightarrow Gx)$ and F and F' are *almost* invariably associated.

Suppose then that I am in possession of such a body of evidence 'e' and that I know that 'Fa' is true and that these form my grounds for believing 'Ga', for which they are, jointly, good evidence. Suppose further that 'Ga' is true, but that it is true not because of Fa [i.e., $\sim (Fa \rightarrow Ga)$] but rather because 'Ha' is true and $Ha \rightarrow Ga$, and that 'Ha' and 'Fa' are not causally connected. Finally, assume that 'Ha' forms no part of my grounds for believing 'Ga.' Then I did not know that Ga. Thus, it would seem that in some cases of knowledge we must require that there be *in fact* a causal connection, not just that we have evidence for it; even as we require that the belief be *in fact* true, not just that we have evidence for its truth.

It may be instructive to compare some general features of the causal counterexamples with the corresponding features of Gettier-type counterexamples. Let 'E' abbreviate 'e & Fa'; 'o' abbreviate 'e & Fa & $(Fa \rightarrow Ga)$' [or, alternatively, 'e & Fa & $(x)(Fx \rightarrow Gx)$']; and 'p' abbreviate 'Ga'. Then, for the causal counterexamples:

    (i) X knows that E

   (ii)   'E' is good evidence for 'o'

  (iii)   'o' entails 'p'

  (iv) X knows that 'E' is good evidence for 'p' [but not in virtue of any knowledge of (ii) and (iii)]

   (v) X believes that p on the basis of the knowledge referred to in (i) and (iv)

  (vi)   'p' is true

 (vii)   'o' is false

(i), (v), (vi), and (vii) have the same form as their Gettier counterparts. But the Gettier counterparts of (ii), (iii), and (iv) are, respectively:

  G-(ii) X knows that 'e' is good evidence for 'o'

 G-(iii) X knows that 'o' entails 'p'

 G-(iv) X knows that 'e' is good evidence of 'p' by virtue of (ii) and (iii)

Thus the Gettier counterexamples require X to use the false statement 'o' to set up the evidential connection between 'e' and 'p', whereas the causal counterexamples do not require X to have even thought about covering laws or statements of causal sufficiency. If my native in the barometer example were queried as to his beliefs about the workings of the barometer, I would have him take a *non fingo hypotheses* attitude. If he is asked whether he doesn't at least have some beliefs about the causal relation between the barometer and the rain, he will either (i) not understand because he does not have the requisite causal concepts, or (ii) reply: "I don't know, I never thought about that. All I know is that, whenever the barometer has fallen, it has rained. So when it falls now, I believe that it will rain." If such answers lead you to believe that my native is not only unsophisticated but also a moron, then so be it. Morons know some things and not others; so the concept of knowledge is applicable to them. In the second example, the pyromaniac did indulge in a little causal reasoning, but a careful examination of the example will show that this is just window dressing.

It should be clear now why the causal counterexamples are not blocked by the conditions that block the Gettier-type counterexamples. The causal counterexamples *do not involve derivative evidentially warranted belief.* Thus the injunction that nonderivative knowledge must be based on nonderivative evidentially warranted belief does not touch them.

Note that, in so far as the words 'sign', 'symptom', and 'indicator' imply the applicability of a causal theory or of general laws, X *may not know* that he is in a situation of type C. He may, for example, conceive of himself as simply making what Carnap calls the "singular predictive inference."[22] However, if someone else (or X himself later) is in possession of such a theory and unearths the relevant facts, he may successfully challenge the claim that X knew that p. Thus, the threat of causal counterexamples ranges far and wide.

The foregoing discussion indicates that, for knowledge of

22 Carnap, *Logical Foundations of Probability,* 2nd ed., p. 568.

type C, we need a new sort of relevance requirement, a requirement of *causal* relevance.[23] In the notation of the examples we have been using, it would seem that we want to require that '$Fa \rightarrow Ga$' be true. It might be suggested that we adopt the more liberal requirement that either '$Fa \rightarrow Ga$' be true or '$Ga \rightarrow Fa$' be true. But this will not do, for the truth of '$Ga \rightarrow Fa$' is not sufficient to block the type of irrelevance that generates the paradoxes. Let us suppose that 'there is a fire in area a' ('Ga') is causally sufficient for 'there is smoke in area a' ('Fa') but not conversely. X sees smoke. Whenever he has seen smoke, he has found fire. Therefore he believes that there is fire in area a. There is. But the smoke that X saw did not result from the fire, but rather from open bottles of ammonia and hydrochloric acid. The fire produced smoke all right, but X didn't see *that* smoke. Thus X didn't know that there was a fire. (It is true that, in the ordinary sense of 'cause', the fire did not cause the smoke that X saw, but that is irrelevant to the point at issue.) This sort of example does not, however, get us into trouble with the stricter requirement that '$Fa \rightarrow Ga$' be true. Let us suppose that 'Z's head has been cut off' ('Fa') is causally sufficient for 'Z is dead' ('Ga'). X is walking along the street and notices Z lying in the gutter, with head severed from body. On the basis of his background knowledge, he arrives at the belief that Z is dead. Sure enough, Z is dead. Now suppose that the sequence of events leading to this pretty scene were as follows: Z was lying in the street, drunk and motionless. Then he died of a heart attack. Finally, a fiend chanced upon the scene and, seeing a man lying in the gutter (but not knowing that he was dead), he whacked off his head. Notice that, in the ordinary sense of 'cause', Z's losing his head was not the cause of death. In fact, it is not even causally connected with his death. *Nevertheless, this would not prevent us*

[23] That a requirement of causal relevance is needed can be demonstrated by simple counterexamples that rely on a totally spurious correlation. I choose the more complex counterexamples to make it clear from the beginning that *just* ruling our spurious correlations would not be sufficient to block all the causal counterexamples.

from granting that X knew that Z was dead. It seems then that
the requirement that '*Fa* → *Ga*' be true, is on the right track.

This requirement, however, is so strong that it blocks many
cases that we would like to call knowledge, along with the
causal paradoxes. In cases of knowledge based on causal signs,
symptoms, and indicators it is almost never the case that the
signs, symptoms, or indicators (or even the signs, symptoms,
and indicators taken together with the background knowledge
of the knower) form a causally sufficient condition for what is
known in the strict sense of 'causally sufficient condition' here
at issue. A closer analysis of the example of the man whose
head has been cut off will serve to illustrate this point. It is
really quite problematical that '*Z*'s head has been cut off' is
causally sufficient for '*Z* is dead' in the strict sense. I know of
no law of nature that is violated under the supposition that *Z*'s
head has been cut off and yet *Z* lives. Furthermore, I doubt
that any such law will ever be discovered, for it seems quite
likely that, given the sort of medical machinery that we shall
have in ten or twenty years together with appropriate plastic
plumbing, a man could live with head severed from body.
Nevertheless, *X*'s knowledge claim holds good, for the example assumes that no such gadgetry was at hand.

What is needed then, is a requirement that is weaker than
(is entailed by but does not entail) the requirement that '*Fa*'
be causally sufficient for '*Ga*' in the strict sense, but yet strong
enough to block the causal paradoxes. The most plausible way
to weaken the requirement and still block the paradoxes is to
reinterpret the arrow as meaning "is a causally sufficient condition for *in the context at hand.*" That is, in the new weak
sense, '*Fa* → *Ga*' will be true if and only if there are statements that truly describe relevant conditions such that the conjunction of these statements with '*Fa*' is causally sufficient for
'*Ga*'. A fully adequate explication of the new weak sense of the
arrow presupposes an analysis of "relevant conditions." And
this task raises problems that I am not prepared to solve. However, these are not *new* problems. The problem of relevant
conditions that is crucial here is exactly the same problem that

is crucial for the analysis of counterfactual conditionals.[24] Our arrow now represents the type of "If . . . then" that is involved in counterfactuals, the difference being that the cases that are important here are cases where the antecedent and consequent are true. Another way of bringing out the connection is to note that inserting the arrow between two true statements yields a true statement if and only if the associated contrapositive counterfactual is licensed (cf. *ibid.*, 14). If we can say "Since the man's head has been cut off, he must be dead," then we can also say "If the man had not been dead, then his head could not have been cut off," and conversely.

Thus, although we do not have a precise explication of the new, weak sense of the arrow, we know enough about how it works for its use in the analysis of knowledge to be not totally unilluminating. I therefore suggest that, for cases of type C, condition (iv): 'p' is true, be replaced by (iv'): '$e \rightarrow p$' is true. [Notice that, once (iv') is added to the conditions, (iv) is redundant.]

Some More Problems with Nonderivative Knowledge: Let us make the reasonable assumption that evidential support is to be graded by some sort of conditional inductive probability. Thus, " 'e' is good evidence of 'p' " is to be understood as "Pr('p' given 'e') is high." Then it must be granted that, even if 'e' is true and Pr('p' given 'e') is high, there may be another true statement 'f' such that Pr('p' given 'e & f') is low. As a result, the existential quantifier in the statement of the conditions for nonderivative knowledge ("There is a statement 'e' such that . . .") will lead to trouble. For suppose that X knows that r_1 & r_2 & . . . & r_n & s_1 & s_2 & . . . s_m, where the r-conjuncts are all evidence for 'p' and the s-conjuncts are all evidence against 'p'. Suppose further that X has derivative knowledge of 'r_1 & r_2 & . . . & r_n' and that this statement is good evidence for 'p'. Clearly, X is going to qualify as knowing some things that he shouldn't know, for people are notori-

[24] See Goodman, *Fact, Fiction, and Forecast* (Cambridge, Mass.: Harvard, 1966), pp. 17–24.

ous for counting the pro evidence and forgetting about the con evidence for something they have an emotional stake in believing. So the other conditions all might very well be met. What is required is that the existential quantifier be replaced by some sort of total-evidence requirement, which guarantees that all relevant pro and con evidence be taken into account. Or, in terms of rules of rational dialectic, we want to legitimize the challenge: "But X knows that f and that $\Pr('p'$ given 'e & f) is not high," and then construct conditions for completely adequate responses that take this new challenging rule into account.

Suppose, then, that we require 'e' to be the conjunction of all those statements that X knows which are relevant to 'p'. This will not do; since, if X really does know 'p', then 'p' itself will be one of those statements. And this would build a vicious circularity into the rules. The difficulty is not obviated by simply modifying the requirement so that 'p' is excluded as a conjunctive part of 'e'. For 'e' may still (and in general will) entail 'p'. But we are here interested in rules for *nonderivative* knowledge. Perhaps we should let 'e' be the maximal conjunction (of statements that X knows that are relevant to 'p') which does not entail p. This suggestion runs into two major difficulties:

(i) There is no guarantee that the definite description in question designates uniquely. (For example, suppose that X knows that q; X knows that $\sim p \supset \sim r$; X knows that $\sim p \supset r$.)

(ii) In assuming that X knows that e, we have made the tacit assumption that, if X knows that e_1 & X knows that e_2 & . . . & X knows that e_n, then X knows that e_1 & e_2 & . . . & e_n. But our treatment of derivative and nonderivative knowledge so far in no way guarantees that this is so.

We might be tempted to answer the second objection as follows: "It is an intuitively obvious and true principle that, if X knows the conjuncts, he knows the conjunction. That this is not a consequence of the foregoing treatment of knowledge, simply exhibits another way in which the foregoing treatment is inadequate." This answer, however, will not hold water. The principle in question is indeed intuitive but nevertheless appears not to be true. Suppose that we can somehow make sense of: $\Pr('p'$ given X's total relevant evidence). Then, no matter what cutoff point we choose for the probability to be called high (unless we say that for the probability to be high it must be equal to 1), it does not follow from $\Pr('p'$ given X's total relevant evidence) is high and $\Pr('q'$ given X's total relevant evidence is high) that $\Pr('p\ \&\ q'$ given X's total relevant evidence is high).[25] We must then say that knowledge is not conjunctive or, to put the matter in a way more pleasing to epistemological skeptics, that, if it is a meaning postulate for knowledge that it be conjunctive, then most nonderivative knowledge isn't really knowledge.

Knowledge and Scientific Explanation: I have no easy answers to the problems raised in the last section. Rather than pursue them further, I shall close this paper by pointing out some interesting similarities between problems of knowledge and problems of scientific explanation and, in particular, between problems of nonderivative knowledge and problems of confirmational explanation.[26]

Problems of scientific explanation can also be given a dialectical twist. The problem of giving conditions for scientific explanation can be thought of as the problem of giving condi-

---

[25] This fact rests on a basic feature of the probability calculus. If I roll a 1000-sided die, the probability that side 1 will not come up is .999; the probability that side 2 will not come up is .999, etc. But the probability of not getting side 1 and not getting side 2 and . . . and not getting side 1000 is 0.

[26] See Scheffler, *The Anatomy of Inquiry* (New York: Knopf, 1963), pp. 31–43; Hempel, "Deductive Nomological vs. Statistical Explanation," in Feigl and Maxwell (eds.), *Minnesota Studies in the Philosophy of Science*, Vol. III (Minneapolis: University of Minnesota Press, 1962), pp. 98–169. Hempel here demonstrates the need for a total-evidence requirement for confirmational explanation and shows that confirmational explanation is nonconjunctive.

tions for a completely adequate response to a Why query
(with 'Why' being taken in the appropriate sense). Suppose
the response 'e' is given to the query 'Why p?'. If the rules of
rational dialectic contain very strong rules of challenging, such
that "'(e & $\sim p$)' is logically possible" is always an appropriate challenge, then it is clear that 'e' will be a completely adequate response if and only if 'e' entails 'p'. (That is, only
deductive explanations would constitute completely adequate
responses.) Such rules of challenging, however, appear to be
overly strong. Suppose that we weaken the challenging rules
so that appropriate challenges are of the form: q & Pr('p' given
'q & e') is not high. Then if the q-statements to be used in
challenging are to be restricted to statements known by the
explainer, we want to say that a completely adequate response
would be one that shows that the probability of 'p' on the
basis of the total relevant evidence had by the explainer is
high. (That is, both deductive explanations and confirmational
explanations would constitute completely adequate responses.)
But the explainer knows that p. Otherwise he would not be
explaining it but rather predicting it or retrodicting it, etc. So
the same problems about total relevant evidence arise. Furthermore, if we remove the restriction on which q-statements can
be used for challenging, then the only completely adequate
responses 'e' will be such that Pr('p' given 'e') = 1. Confirmational explanation is not, in general, conjunctive for the same
reason that nonderivative knowledge isn't. Finally, both the
Gettier-type counterexamples and the causal counterexamples
can be transferred with full force to contexts of confirmational
explanation.

It is to be hoped that a recognition of the common ground
shared by the problems of the explication of knowledge and
the explication of scientific explanation will facilitate their
solution, and that the dialectical approach[27] will provide a useful perspective for their analysis.

[27] The dialectical approach has many other interesting applications.
For instance, the parallel between concerns which motivated the use of
the dialectical approach in this paper, and concerns at the heart of
ethics should be obvious.

Peter Unger

An Analysis of
Factual Knowledge*

I intend to provide an analysis of human factual knowledge, in
other words, an analysis of what it is for a man to know that
something is the case. I try to capture the conception of human
factual knowledge that ordinary knowledgeable humans do in
fact employ in making commonsensical judgments about the
presence or absence of such knowledge. My analysis will depart most radically from all previously offered analyses and
will, I think, be all the better for this departure.

I. The Presence of Knowledge and the Absence of Accident

In a recent critical paper,[1] after arguing to refute the idea that
knowledge of most contingent matters must be based on ex-

From *The Journal of Philosophy*, 65, 6 (March 21, 1968), 157–170. Reprinted by permission of the author and *The Journal of Philosophy*.

* I thank The University of Wisconsin for providing me with generous
financial support during the summer of 1966, when I wrote much of this
paper, and for providing me, during the spring of 1966, with the students
in my Problems of Knowledge course, about half of whom made helpful
contributions to my thinking on the matters with which the paper is
concerned. Additional support (not of a financial kind) was provided,
not unusually, by Saul A. Kripke and Michael A. Slote, in this case,
especially by Mr. Slote; I thank them both for their helpful criticism and
guarded approval, retaining full responsibility for that on which I made
them spend their valuable time and efforts.

[1] "Experience and Factual Knowledge," *The Journal of Philosophy*,
LXIV, 5 (March 16, 1967): 152–173.

perience, I put forward the following (there numbered 12.1, page 172) as providing a logically necessary condition of when a man's belief is an instance of knowledge:

(0) For any sentential value of p, a man's belief that p is an instance of knowledge only if it is not an accident that the man's belief is true.

Speaking of a man's belief as being an instance of knowledge may be too unnatural; at any rate it is not a very ordinary sort of thing to do. And, in the end, we are not so interested in when a man's belief might be an instance of knowledge, as we are in when a man might know that something is so. Thus, motivated by a consideration of (0), I now assert as a unified and univocal analysis of human factual knowledge:

(1) For any sentential value of p, (at a time t) a man knows that p if and only if (at t) it is not at all accidental that the man is right about its being the case that p.

To speak most clearly and correctly, a reference to specific times should be an explicit part of any adequate analysis of human knowledge. At one time it may be at least somewhat accidental that a man is right about a certain matter, although at another time it is not at all accidental that he is right. Thus, a man may believe that there is a rosebush on his vast estate simply because a servant told him so and convinced him of that. The servant did not know of the existence of any rosebush and only convinced the man for amusement, thinking, indeed, that he had got his employer to believe something false. However, unbeknownst to the servant there was a rosebush in a far corner of the estate. One day the man may ride into that corner of the estate. We may suppose that he sees the rosebush. Before he sees the bush, it is entirely accidental that the estate owner has been right about there being a rosebush on his estate; when he sees the bush, it first becomes the case that it is not at all accidental that he is right about the matter.

This is when the man first knows that his estate is so blessed. Again, and in contrast, a man who holds no opinion on the matter may see a rosebush and so first come to know and to be right that it is in a certain place. While he still has some but no very strong memory of the matter, he may believe that the rosebush is there and may have this belief as a result of his remembering that it is there. While he has this belief, a friend who has no knowledge of the rosebush, who simply wants to convince the man that there is a rosebush in the aforementioned place, may tell the man in most convincing and memorable terms that he, the friend, saw the rosebush there. When he hears the friend's story the man holds his belief about the rosebush both because he has seen it and remembers that it is there, and also because of the friend's story; either then being sufficient to ensure his then holding that belief. At this time the man does know; for, because he originally saw the bush, it is then not at all accidental that he is right about the location of the bush. Still later, the man may still believe that the rosebush is in the proper location but only because his friend so convincingly told him so. His originally seeing the bush will then be not at all responsible for his holding the (correct) belief. At this point, the man no longer knows; for at the time in question it is false that it is not at all accidental that the man is right about the matter. Indeed, at this time it is very much an accident that he is right about its being the case that the rosebush is in the place in question, and thus it is clear that at the time in question the man does not know the location of the bush.

It is essential, then, that we think of a man as knowing something *at a certain time* and say that *at that time* it is not at all accidental that he is right. With this understanding firmly in mind, we need not always refer to times in our subsequent discussion, and, to make matters easier, we often will not do so.

II. Irrelevant Accidents

What we properly regard as an accident, or as accidental, does appear to depend upon our various interests, as well as upon other things. Thus, even in the most physically deterministic universe imaginable, automobile accidents may occur, and it may be largely accidental that one man, rather than another, is successful in his competitive business enterprise. To provide an analysis of when something is an accident, or somewhat accidental, is more than I am (now) capable of doing. Nor can I show in any helpful detail how our notion of an accident, or of something's being accidental, may be used to express or reflect the various interests we might have. Thus, I will rely on a shared intuitive understanding of these notions.

In my analysis of human factual knowledge, a complete absence of the accidental is claimed, not regarding the occurrence or existence of the fact known nor regarding the existence or abilities of the man who knows, but only as regards a certain relation concerning the man and the fact. Thus, it may be accidental that p and a man may know that p, for it may nevertheless be that it is not at all accidental that the man is right about its being the case that p. In other words, a man may know about an auto accident: when the car accidentally crashes into the truck, a bystander who observes what is going on may well know that the car crashed into the truck and accidentally did so. He will know just in case it is not at all accidental that he is right about its being the case that the car crashed into the truck and accidentally did so. Nor do I claim that there must be nothing accidental in the way that a man comes to know that p. Thus, a man may overhear his employer say that he will be fired and he may do so quite by accident, not intending to be near his employer's office or to gain any information from his employer. Though it may be an accident that the man came to know that he will be fired, and it may be somewhat accidental that he knows this to be so, nevertheless, from the time that he hears and onward, it may well be not at all accidental that the man is right about its being the case that he will be fired. Thus, he may know, whether by accident or not.

Of all the things that a man knows, none is more certainly known by him than the fact of his own existence. Thus, it must be most obvious that a man who, at a certain time, exists or is alive only as a matter of some accident may, even at that time, know about various matters of fact; he may, for instance, most certainly know that he exists. Though it may be largely accidental that he exists or is alive, it may be not at all accidental that he is right about various matters of fact: (indeed, necessarily, should he sincerely hold that he then existed, it would be not at all accidental that he was right about that matter). These points can perhaps be made more clear by our considering the following simple story: Suppose that a man is looking at a turtle and even seeing that the turtle is crawling on the ground. This man may know that the turtle is crawling on the ground (and will in that he sees that it is); for because he is using his eyes (and because of other things as well), it may be that at that time it is not at all accidental that the man is right about its being the case that the turtle is crawling on the ground. However, suppose further that just at this time, or immediately before it, a heavy rock would have fallen on the man and would have killed him then and there, smashing him to smithereens, but for the occurrence of an accidental happening which prevents the rock from falling and allows him to remain alive. Say, all of three terrible people who were pushing the rock that was to fall were themselves, coincidentally and simultaneously, hit on the head by three independently falling bricks and were killed upon impact. Each of the bricks, quite independently of the others, just happened to fall loose from an ancient wall of which they all were a part. Thus, quite by accident, all three of the terrible rock pushers were killed, and the turtle watcher's life was spared, perhaps only until some later time. On these suppositions, it is indeed quite an accident that the turtle watcher is alive at the time he sees the turtle crawling on the ground before him. Yet, at that time, it is not at all accidental that he is right about its being the case that there is a turtle on the ground. And at that time, as we have supposed, the turtle watcher knows that there is a turtle crawling there upon the ground. These are the judgments that common sense and good sense would make about our case.

Thus, it may be not at all accidental that a man is right about a certain matter, even though it is very much an accident that he then exists or is alive. Once we are clear about this, we can more fully appreciate the ability of my analysis to explain the cogency of Cartesian examples. Though it be accidental that a certain man exist, yet necessarily if he thinks that he exists, it is not at all accidental that he is right about the matter. An unwanted and accidental child, pursued by hapless rock pushers all his life, may grow up to know more than any of his brothers or sisters. He may do so even on my analysis of human factual knowledge, whether he fancy himself a Cartesian skeptic or whether he be entirely unconcerned with such philosophical profundities.

III. Accidents and Phenomena of Chance

The condition of my analysis is stronger than the necessary condition most naturally suggested by my earlier statement (0) and explicitly given by the following:

> (2) For any sentential value of p, a man knows that p if and only if it is not an accident that the man is right about its being the case that p.

That such strength is required, that the weaker condition of (2) is not sufficient, can be most readily seen by considering our thought about phenomena of chance. Such a consideration will show, I think, how only our stronger condition, and none such as that of (2), adequately reflects tensions that often exist in the application of the concept of knowledge.

Let us, then, suppose a standard and simple sort of example: a man knows that a deck of cards contains ninety-nine white cards, one black card, and no others. He also knows that the cards have just been well shuffled and fairly so. On the basis of this knowledge, he concludes, as is his custom, that it is likely that the top card is white. Thus he may come to believe that the top card is white, and we may suppose him to do so. Let us further suppose that the top card is white: we are supposing that the man's belief is correct, that he is right about its being the case that the top card is white. The only reason that he has this (correct) belief is that he has reasoned in a certain way on the basis of the knowledge that we have supposed him to have. Now once we have made all these suppositions, we have supposed, not only that the man is right, but also, and with equal clarity, that it is not an accident that he is right about the matter. But, in contrast, it is *not* entirely clear that it is not at all accidental that the man is right. But, equally, it is *not* clear that it is *false* that it is not at all accidental that he is. In other words, there is a tension in the application of our analytic condition to the probabilistic case presented. This same tension is also in evidence when we consider the application of our concept of factual knowledge. For in the simple case presented, it is *neither* clear that the man does know *nor* clear that he does not. The suppositions neither allow nor yield any decisive answer as to whether the man knows the color of the top card.

The magnitude of the numbers involved may help to further our willingness to say that the man knows, to apply our conconcept of knowledge. But sheer consideration of number will not remove the tension entirely. Thus, were there a billion white cards, and only one of another color, we are more ready to say that the man who bets that the top card is white knows full well that he will win (assuming of course that he will win). Still, we may also find ourselves saying that he cannot really know that he has won until the color of the card is actually revealed. Similarly, such an increase in the chances furthers our readiness to apply our analytic condition, to say that it is not at all accidental that the man is right (assuming of course that he is right). But again, and equally I think, our willingness here is not so complete as it might be. Perhaps it is not really true, after all, that it is not at all accidental that he is right, even when such large numbers are involved. Thus, a consideration of our thought about such simple probabilistic cases gives some further support to the claim that our analytic condition mirrors well our concept of factual knowledge.

We may gain yet further support, I think, by considering the way in which our thought about more highly structured cases compares with what we think about such unstructured cases of the most simple probabilistic kind. In contrast to the first case of the card deck, let us consider the following, more structured sort of case, where considerations of probability enter rather less directly: a man is performing a hundred problems in addition and checking his answers by an independent arithmetic method. These problems each involve his adding three different numbers, each between 10 and 100. There is nothing mysterious here: the man uses the normal paper-and-pencil methods for both adding and checking. He always expresses the numbers in the decimal system, in the familiar arabic notation. Suppose the man, like most other men, characteristically to make only one mistake unspotted, and eventually to add and check correctly in ninety-nine of the hundred cases. And suppose him in *each* case to think the answer correct (though we may allow that he may not think he has been correct in *all* cases). Then, with respect to each problem that he worked and checked correctly, our common-sense judgment would be that he knew what the answer was. Having worked the problem correctly, he would know, for example, that 134 is the sum of 32 and 49 and 53. And equally, the common-sense attitude still prevailing, there is no doubt but that we should say that it is not at all accidental that the man is right about the sum. Such tension as was present in the purely probabilistic case of the card deck, is now absent from our judgment—both as regards our concept of knowledge and as regards our analytic condition. Exactly why cases like that involving fallible addition should differ so markedly from cases of pure probability is a deep question that cries out for further analysis and greater understanding. But though our understanding of these matters is presently quite limited, we may recognize that there are between the two sorts of cases just considered, notable differences in our willingness to apply our concept of factual knowledge. Even here, where my analysis leads us to no very important increase in our understanding of the relevant matters, we may say that the analysis has received some notable support.[2]

IV. Justification, Evidence, and Knowledge

My analysis of human factual knowledge differs markedly from those analyses in which an attempt is made to consider such knowledge as some sort of justified true belief. Indeed, according to my analysis a man may know something without his being in any way justified in believing that it is so. And my analysis does not require, as does that of A. J. Ayer,[3] that

(3) For any sentential value of p, a man knows that p only if the man has the right to be sure that p.

It also disagrees with Roderick Chisholm's claim[4] that

(4) For any sentential value of p, a man knows that p only if the man has adequate evidence that p.

Let us consider a straightforward example which upsets these claims most decisively, and shows that no sort of justification is ever a necessary condition for knowledge. Thus, we may better understand my analysis by seeing how it conflicts with this other, more traditional view.

The example, which I first adduced in my aforementioned essay against empiricism, concerns a certain gypsy, one who, we must conclude, knows things of which others are ignorant. Our gypsy has been brought up to accept the messages of a

---

[2] I have been much influenced on these matters and others that I have been writing about, by discussions with Robert Nozick and Michael Anthony Slote.

[3] *The Problem of Knowledge* (London: Macmillan, 1956), ch. I, "Philosophy and Knowledge," pp. 31–35, esp. p. 35. [Pp. 11–15 of the present volume. Ed.]

[4] *Perceiving: A Philosophical Study* (Ithaca, N.Y.: Cornell, 1957), ch. I, "Epistemic Terms," esp. p. 16.

certain crystal ball that he inherited from his family. Owing to forces in nature which no one understands, the ball always gives a correct report on any matter on which it provides a message. And, because of certain loyalties and beliefs instilled by his upbringing, the gypsy never checks up on the ball in any way whatever. We shall, indeed, suppose the gypsy to believe, what he inferred from what he learned later in life, that the ball will almost never give a correct report. But though the gypsy has this (false) general belief, which we may suppose him to be justified in having, when it comes to any particular matter, he cannot help but believe the message of the ball. Moreover, these acquired beliefs he holds most insistently though he is unable to provide any reasonable defense of these beliefs when challenged and is even wholly unconcerned with whether he is reasonable or not in holding them. We may even suppose that, despite his unreasonable attitudes and the lack of adequate evidence for his beliefs, the gypsy is entirely confident about the truth of each report despite his knowledge of its source and his belief about the general unreliability of the source. Where the fact that p is reported by the ball, on these suppositions, the gypsy does not have adequate evidence that p, and especially so when we further suppose him to have a wealth of evidence for thinking it false that p. Does the gypsy then have the right to be sure that p? Plainly not, unless everyone has the right to be sure of anything that is true. Such are the effects of the gypsy's early upbringing and certain later happenings.

But it does appear that, in the present case, the effects are not wholly and simply unfortunate ones. Owing to the gypsy's early upbringing and the operation of the crystal ball, the gypsy does have knowledge of those matters on which the ball delivers a report. This fact may be made especially clear by supposing that the gypsy's parents knew, by observational check or by some other means, that the ball gave only correct reports. On this basis they raised their gypsy child to accept unquestioningly the reports of the ball, whether these be of a pictorial sort or whether expressed in some sort of unusual writing. Thus, this gypsy, though he is only unreasonable in believing that p, knows that p, where the report that p is a report of the ball that the gypsy accepts. Though our gypsy does not satisfy the conditions of (3) or (4), he does have factual knowledge. For it is, after all, not at all accidental that he is right about the relevant matters. Thus we can see how my analysis conflicts with the fundamental claims of leading contemporary analysts, and how only my analysis survives this conflict intact.

As my analysis dictates, we must give up the idea that factual knowledge is any sort of justified true belief, or anything of the like. But even so, we may obtain both a better understanding of and further support for the analysis by examining another idea, one that derives from the attempt to understand our knowledge in this traditional way. This derivative idea is that a belief that represents knowledge on someone's part cannot be based on grounds that are entirely false. This derivative idea comes from a consideration of the standard sort of argument to show that epistemically justified true belief is not logically *sufficient* for factual knowledge. According to this standard argument, a man justifiedly deduces from justified beliefs of his that are entirely false, a true conclusion which he accepts on the basis of the deduction. Thus, by believing the conclusion, the man has an epistemically justified belief which, though true, represents no knowledge on his part.[5] It may be thought, then, that this justified true belief fails to be knowledge simply because it is based on grounds that are false. We might then require of a belief that some of its grounds be true, if the belief represent knowledge.

But such a requirement would be too strong. There are various examples in terms of which this may be seen. I should most like to adduce the main example of my aforementioned essay. In this example, knowledgeable scientists successfully

[5] This standard argument is most influentially stated by Edmund L. Gettier in his "Is Justified True Belief Knowledge?," *Analysis*, xxiii.6, n.s. 96 (June 1963): 121–123 [pp. 35–38 of the present volume. Ed.] and it is earlier suggested by Bertrand Russell in *The Problems of Philosophy* (New York: Oxford, 1912), ch. xiii, "Knowledge, Error, and Probable Opinion," esp. p. 131 ff.

duplicate a person who the scientists know to have a lot of important factual knowledge. They do this in order that there be more people who have this knowledge. The duplicate knows various things, say, various facts of physics. And we can now better say why he does: he knows because it is not at all accidental that the duplicate is right about these physical matters. But the beliefs that represent this knowledge on the part of the duplicate, all have as grounds beliefs that are entirely false. The duplicate, just like a normal scientist, bases his beliefs about the physical world on beliefs about his own personal history and experience: about what he has seen and read, about the experiments he has performed and heard about, and so on. But the duplicate has not done any of these things. Thus, these constructed duplicates, which satisfy the condition of my analysis, show that a belief may represent knowledge though it be based on grounds that are themselves entirely false.

Why, then, is there a lack of knowledge on the part of the man whose justified true belief is, in a simple and straightforward way, deduced from and based on grounds that are entirely false? The answer is, I think, that given by my analysis. Generally, with such a man, it is entirely accidental that he is right about the matter in question, whereas, for him to know, it must be quite the opposite. It must be not at all accidental that he is right about the matter.

In connection with our simple answer, we may note that there are other ways of seeing that justified true belief need not ensure factual knowledge. With such ways, no false belief is attributed to the man in question, and thus his failure to know is most clearly unrelated to his having any false grounds. One such way, it is interesting to note, is suggested by the card-deck examples we examined in the previous section. There, we noted that, with a very high proportion of white cards to black, it is not easy to tell or decide whether the man knows the top card to be white. But where we have, say, eighty-five white cards and fifteen black ones, it is *clear* that the man who reasons to the belief that the top card is white does not know the card to be white. On the other hand, it is also clear that the man is epistemically justified in believing the card to be white. Thus, though this man has no relevant false beliefs and though he reasons in no faulty manner, his epistemically justified true belief fails to represent knowledge. Again, the result is explained by my analysis: this man does not know because it is false that it is not at all accidental that he is right. So it is of interest that, in yet another way, a consideration of purely probabilistic cases lends support to my analysis while rendering it still more implausible that factual knowledge be some sort of justified true belief or, for that matter, anything of the like.

V. The Imprecision of the Concept of Knowledge

No doubt, any attempted analysis of factual knowledge will fail to take account of every imaginable case and example as nicely as one might wish. But, then, our concept of knowledge is itself not so exact with every imaginable case as one might wish it to be. Primarily in connection with certain matters peculiar to his own account of factual knowledge, Bertrand Russell warns against our having unrealistic expectations:

> But in fact 'knowledge' is not a precise conception: . . . A very precise definition, therefore, should not be sought, since any such definition must be more or less misleading (*op. cit.*, p. 134).

Thus, though various examples may be brought to refute a putatively adequate analysis, whether such examples show the analysis to be inadequate is not always a very easy matter to decide.

Having expressed these thoughts, I will now put forward what has occurred to me as the example most likely to incline someone to reject the analysis that I offer. As might be expected, the example apparently could be used to show that the condition of my analysis is too weak, to show, that is, that at a certain time it might be not at all accidental that a man is right about its being the case that p and, even so, at that time he may not know that p. But I think that when this example is judged with impartiality and care, it is seen not to present any problem for my analysis of human factual knowledge. Indeed, such careful scrutiny, if anything, reveals that, when most clearly understood, the apparently damaging example actually may lend support to my analysis.

The example that I offer involves what might be called the fulfillment of a man's expectation about the future being brought about as a result of the man's having that expectation. Such happenings can, of course, occur in various ways, but rather than attempt to consider the entire variety, let us turn directly to the most bizarre sort of example, which is apparently most troublesome. Let us think, then, of a man who has a dream, and dreams that a certain horse will win a certain race. The man that I imagine generally believes only some of the things that he dreams will happen, and those that he believes simply as a result of a dream, he mumbles audibly upon awakening. Upon awakening from his dream about the horse race, the man mumbled that Schimmelpenninck, one of the horses to run in the 1965 Kentucky Derby, would be the winner of that race. Now, whenever our man awakes, he is wakened by his friend, who sees to it that the man has time to do his morning exercises. The friend knows that whatever the man mumbles upon awakening is what he has just dreamed about the future and thus believes will happen. The friend thus knows each of the man's beliefs that come to him simply as a result of dreaming, and he knows of each of these that it is the product of a dream. Hence, in particular, the friend knows that the man believes that Schimmelpenninck will win the 1965 Kentucky Derby, and he knows that the man acquired this belief simply as a result of his having an appropriate dream about that horse race. The friend, that morning, immediately decides to ensure the truth (or correctness) of his friend's belief; he resolves that the dreamer's belief be true. Now, the friend is an eminent veterinarian with access to all racing stables, and so he drugs all of Schimmelpenninck's competitors, endeavoring to fulfill the resolution that he made. I suppose that in this way the friend ensures that Schimmelpenninck is the winner of the 1965 Kentucky Derby; among other things, I here assume that Schimmelpenninck does finish first and that the veterinarian's activities are not detected. We may even suppose that once the veterinarian had made up his mind, it was no longer a matter of any chance which horse would win the race. In short, we may even suppose that the veterinarian knows that Schimmelpenninck will win. It is not very important here whether we suppose that without the doctor's intervention the horse would not have won, or whether we suppose the opposite, that the horse would have won anyway. In either case, the veterinarian knows the winner of the race. But the dreamer has no knowledge of the winner, for he always believes that Schimmelpenninck will win simply because he has a dream, a dream relevantly unconnected with the race to be run, and he never does in any way gain any relevant information.

It is clear that, on our suppositions, the dreamer does not know at any time. Yet, it may appear that, after the veterinarian makes his resolve or after he drugs the horse's competitors, it is not at all accidental that the dreamer is right about its being the case that Schimmelpenninck is the winner. But such appearances, I fear, would be most deceptive. Were it truly the case that at the relevant times it is not at all accidental that the dreamer is right, then we should have to make much stronger suppositions about our case than those we have made. Indeed, we should then have to make just such suppositions as render the çase one most plausibly described as one in which the dreamer does know. To see that all of this is so, let us ask some questions of the presented case, questions which make it most dubious to suppose that the case is one which is correctly described by saying that it is not at all accidental that the dreamer is right about the outcome of the race.

The essential accidentality will not be fully brought out by asking what we should say were the veterinarian to make his resolve, not after his learning of the dreamer's acquisition of belief, but in advance of such information. To see this clearly, we may suppose the contrasting situation, that the doctor does make his resolve in advance, even long before the dreamer has the appropriate dream, and that he resolves that should his friend ever dream that a certain horse would win a certain running of the Kentucky Derby, he, the veterinarian, would ensure that his friend's belief be true. For even with such a supposition, the circumstances of which are unknown to the dreamer, we may ask: First, why did the veterinarian make just that particular resolve, which is still a rather specific one, and not some other one, or, better, some very general resolve whose fulfillment would entail the fulfillment of many particular resolves he might well make? And second, would the doctor be able to ensure the truth of other sorts of dream-produced beliefs that his friend might have, beliefs about future fluctuations of the stock market, future moon-rocket launchings, earthquakes, elections, and eclipses? These questions do, I think, bring out the large amount of accidentality that remains concerning the relevant matter, even after we have supposed that the veterinarian made his resolve long in advance of the particular dream or in advance of information of it. But, in contrast to the case so far considered, we may make suppositions that are quite extreme, and so rule out rather clearly any accidentality about the dreamer's being right about the subject of his opinion: We will imagine that the earth and all the life upon it were originally created by an extremely powerful and knowledgeable being. This being's chief fascination was with ensuring that a man's beliefs be true in case he acquired those beliefs simply as a result of a dream. In line with his most important desires, the being so created everyone that no man would ever have a dream-produced belief that conflicted with that of any other man; thus the being ensured that it be possible that he ensure the truth of every man's dream-produced belief about the future, for he also saw to it that no man would come to have any inconsistent beliefs simply as the result of a dream. Further, as the being well knew, it was well within his power to ensure the truth of any such belief that would ever actually be held. And the being, acting reasonably with respect to his chief fascination, proceeded to do what he knew to be well within his power. Now, though some philosophers might think otherwise, it strikes me as rather clear that a fair employment of our shared conception of factual knowledge dictates that, in such a world as this, the being has ensured that a man's dreams are a source of knowledge for the man (just in case the man believes that what he dreams about the future is the way that things will be). We have, then, presented a rather clear case of knowledge of the future which is of the relevant kind, enabling us to give an answer to what appeared to be the gravest problem that would befall my analysis of human factual knowledge. Happily, this example is quite in accord with that analysis, for it is on such extreme suppositions as those we have just made that it is most clear that, at the relevant time, it is not at all accidental that the man is right about the subject of his opinion.

Complete satisfaction with our extreme case allows us better to understand cases that are not so extreme, and thus not so clear. For example, we can now better understand and appreciate the following sort of case, one that lies somewhere between the last two we have considered: We suppose that a powerful and knowledgeable man makes a longstanding resolve that all of his dreaming friend's appropriate beliefs about the outcomes of all sporting events would be correct, and that the man succeeds in fulfilling this resolve, just as he knew that he would. About such a situation, we should not be so very disinclined to judge that the powerful man ensured that his friend's dreams were a source of knowledge for that man (just when he believes that what he dreams about the future is the way that things will be). Just so, about such a situation, we should be equally and not so very disinclined to judge that the powerful man ensured that at the relevant times it was not at all accidental that the dreamer was right about the subjects of his dream-produced beliefs.

Our putative counterexample, about the dreamer and his friend the veterinarian, has been shown to present problems that are only apparent. Indeed, by pursuing further these merely apparent difficulties, we have encountered relevantly similar cases that lend support to my analysis of human factual knowledge. Now, in all such cases of knowledge, as we suppose that the knower is wholly unaware both of the agent who makes it happen that he knows and of any happenings that help explain his knowledge, we may say that he does not know why he knows various things about the future, or at least that he knows almost nothing about why he knows. But still, should the man in such an example believe that he knows, this belief having as its source the same process of dreaming as does the belief that is supposed to represent knowledge on the part of the man, then, so far as I can see, there is no good reason for denying that the man knows *that* he knows, though he may lack completely knowledge of why he knows. Of course, we do know why the man knows; we know that a powerful agent makes it happen that at the relevant time it is not at all accidental that the man is right.

Apparent problems now appear to be resolved entirely, this resolution affording further support for my analysis of human factual knowledge.

William W. Rozeboom

Why I Know So Much More Than You Do

What does it mean to say that person X "knows" that p? With a unanimity remarkable for philosophers, it is generally agreed that for this to be true, it must obtain that

(a) p is the case,
(b) X believes that p, and
(c) X is justified in believing p.

Whether conditions (a)–(c) jointly suffice for X to know that p, however, has recently been disputed by several writers.[1] I

From *American Philosophical Quarterly*, 4, 4 (1967), 281–290. Reprinted by permission of the author and Basil Blackwell.

[1] See Gettier [23], Clark [18], Sosa [42], Saunders and Champawat [41], Lehrer [33], and Harman [25]. [Numbers in brackets refer to entries in the Selected Bibliography on pages 221–224. Ed.] The justified-true-belief view of knowledge has been well stated by Ayer [2, ch. i], Chisholm [3, ch. i], and Woozley [7, ch. 8] (though Woozley rashly puts the justification condition as having *evidence* for what one knows), and recently defended in one respect or another by Arner [11], Saunders [40], and Harrison [26]. While condition (b) has occasionally been disputed on the rather foolish ground that "believes" is sometimes understood to imply "does not feel sure of," the necessity of (a) and (b) for knowing that p is essentially noncontroversial. The status of (c), however, is more problematic. Armstrong [1, p. 120], Malcolm [6, p. 225ff.], and Sosa [42] contend from an overly narrow equating of "justification" with "evidence" that justification is not always requisite to

shall attempt to show that these doubts are unfounded, and that the *justified true belief* analysis of knowledge (hereafter referred to as the "JTB thesis") is indeed adequate. But I shall then proceed to agitate related perplexities about the concept of "knowledge" and conclude with a possibly heretical suggestion about its continued usefulness for technical epistemology.

I

Estranged from his wife and beset by financial troubles, John Duosmith has become conspicuously despondent. Today, a man's body is found in Duosmith's hotel room with Duosmith's revolver in its hand, a bullet therefrom in its head, and a suicide note signed by Duosmith on the table. Mrs. Duosmith identifies the body as that of her husband, pointing out his characteristic birthmark, the private details of their recent quarrel cited in the note, and so on for many other items which make it overwhelmingly evident to Mrs. Duosmith that the corpse of John Duosmith lies before her, and hence that her husband is dead.

And John Duosmith is indeed dead. But what has happened is this: Last night, Duosmith received a secret visit from his identical twin brother Jim, a petty criminal whose existence John had concealed from his wife and who now begged John to hide him from certain colleagues seeking retribution for something Jim had done. Seeing a chance to make a new life for himself, John shot his brother and arranged the scene to

---

knowing. In contrast, Gettier [23], Clark [18], Lehrer [33], and Harman [25] accept the necessity of (c) for knowing p but deny its sufficiency given (a, b), while Saunders and Champawat [41] question the possibility of finding *any* set of conditions which are necessary and sufficient for all instances of "knowledge."

Though not strictly addressed to the analysis of "knowing," recent discussion by Chisholm [4], Brown [15], and Saunders [39] concerning self-justifying beliefs, and Hintikka's [5] widely acclaimed exploration of the modal logic of knowledge and belief are also background context for the present work.

appear as though he, John, had killed himself. But as John left the hotel, he was spotted by Jim's pursuers who, mistaking him for his twin, promptly executed their plans for Jim's demise. So John Duosmith is dead while his wife, for the best of reasons, also believes this to be so.

But does Mrs. Duosmith *know* that her husband is dead? Mr. Gettier and others[2] say "No," and my own linguistic intuition agrees with this judgment. The force of this and similar examples cited by Gettier *et seq.* is drawn from the principle that true beliefs grounded upon false premises do not count as knowledge, no matter how reasonable those premisses may themselves be under the circumstances. That is,

(A) If person X believes *p*—justifiably—only because he believes *q*, while he justifiably believes *q* on the basis of evidence *e*, then *q* as well as *p* must be the case if X's belief in *p* is to qualify as "knowledge."

Consequently, if *p* is true while *q* is false in such a case, as apparently illustrated by the Duosmith episode and Gettier's examples, it follows that a person may justifiably believe true proposition *p* and still not *know* that *p*. Now in fact, these examples do *not* show this, nor can the JTB thesis ever be threatened by principle (A). But before I point out why this is so, it is best to undermine confidence that linguistic intuition can be trusted to provide a sound interpretation of cases like these.

II

It is Sunday afternoon, and Mrs. Jones is on her way to borrow an egg from her neighbor, Mrs. Togethersmith. She fears that she may be too late, however, for she is aware that every Sunday afternoon for the past several years, the Togethersmith family—Mr. and Mrs. Togethersmith and their two children—has gone for a drive in the country. As she steps outside, Mrs.

[2] See n.1.

Jones sees the Togethersmith car departing with Mr. Togethersmith at the wheel, and thinks to herself, "Pity, there she goes."
Mrs. Jones believes that Mrs. Togethersmith is driving away
because, for excellent reasons, she believes that the entire
Togethersmith family is in the departing car. But in fact, while
Mrs. Togethersmith, her husband, and one of their children
are indeed in the departing car, the other Togethersmith child
is on this one occasion attending a friend's birthday party.
Insomuch as it is not true that the entire Togethersmith family
is driving away, is Mrs. Jones's justified true belief, that Mrs.
Togethersmith is driving away, *knowledge?* Principle (A)
appears to deny this, since Mrs. Jones arrived at her true belief
about Mrs. Togethersmith by means of a justified but false
belief about the whereabouts of the entire Togethersmith
family. But the falsehood here seems so *irrelevant.* For "The
entire Togethersmith family is driving away" is equivalent to
the conjunction "Mrs. Togethersmith is driving away, Mr.
Togethersmith is driving away, and all the Togethersmith children are driving away," the components of which are supported by Mrs. Jones's evidence just as well separately as
conjoined—in fact, it is difficult to say whether Mrs. Jones's
belief about Mrs. Togethersmith derives from her belief about
the Togethersmith family as a whole, or is a part-cause of it. In
any event, linguistic intuition is disposed to deny that the
absence of one Togethersmith child from the departing family
car disqualifies Mrs. Jones's justified true belief about Mrs.
Togethersmith's departure as an instance of knowledge.

But if so, what about Mr. Jones, who, wanting a 12-inch
board, measures one with his new tape rule, obtains a 10-inch
reading, and concludes "That's too small," when the tape rule
is defective and this board is really 11 inches? (We assume
that Jones has had much past experience with tape rules, all
of which amply warrants his trust in the present reading.) Mr.
Jones's justified belief, that this board is under 12 inches, is
true even though it is derived from his false justified belief that
this board is 10 inches. Since intuitively this case is no different
in kind from Mrs. Duosmith's belief about her dead husband,
we should deny that Jones *knows* this board is less than 12

inches. Yet "This board is 10 inches" is equivalent to the conjunction "This board is under 12 inches, this board is at least 10 inches, and this board is not between 10 and 12 inches," only the last component of which is false while its first component requires for its justification only a proper part of the evidence which supports Jones's belief in the whole conjunction. So by formal parallel, it might also seem that Mr. Jones's conclusion that this board is undersize should not be epistemically inferior to Mrs. Jones's belief in Mrs. Togethersmith's departure.

More intensive analysis of these two cases would show not so much that one or both violate principle (A) as that when a person's justified true belief p is accompanied by a justified false belief q, it may well prove troublesome to decide whether or not his belief in p is related to his belief in q in such fashion that the falsity of the latter should disqualify the former as knowledge. That this is in general a failure of conception, not just an insufficiency of data concerning the believer's detailed reasoning, is shown by the following more sophisticated example.

Dr. Pillsmith, a competent practitioner of medicine, is well aware that:

(1) Among persons who have not been vaccinated against Hypofluvia, 999,999 out of a million who show symptoms S are afflicted with this disease,

(2) Among vaccinated persons showing symptoms S, only one in ten is afflicted with Hypofluvia,

(3) Only one person in a million showing symptoms S has been vaccinated against Hypofluvia,

and that consequently,[3]

(4) More than 999,998 persons in a million who show symptoms S are afflicted with Hypofluvia.

[3] Since for any three attributes A, B, and C, $\Pr(A|B) = \Pr(C|B) \times \Pr(A|BC) + \Pr(\overline{C}|B) \times \Pr(A|B\overline{C}) > [1-\Pr(C|B)] \times \Pr(A|B\overline{C})$.

Attempting to diagnose the condition of his latest patient, Dr. Pillsmith observes that

(5) Philip Blotely shows symptoms S,

and, lacking further information about Blotely's medical history, infers unhesitatingly from (1)–(5) both that

(6) Philip Blotely has not been vaccinated against Hypofluvia

and that

(7) Philip Blotely has Hypofluvia.

Now it so happens that Blotely was, in fact, vaccinated against Hypofluvia, but has contracted it just the same. So Pillsmith's diagnosis (7) is both justified and true—but is it knowledge? At first it might seem that the falsity of (6) thwarts this, for were Pillsmith to surmise the truth of Blotely's vaccination, his knowledge of (2) and (5) would prevent him from justifiedly accepting (7). Yet (6) is at the same time irrelevant to the diagnosis in that Pillsmith can get to (7) from (5) and (1)-(3) by way of (4) without ever considering whether or not Blotely has been vaccinated. And if Pillsmith does make his diagnosis in this way, must (6) still be true if Pillsmith's justified belief, that Blotely has Hypofluvia, is to count as knowledge? Surely not, since falsehood (6) takes no part in the inference. Yet we can also argue that justification of (7) by (5) and (1)-(3) via (4) implicitly presupposes the truth of (6), for derivation of (4) from (1)-(3) argues in effect: Given any person with symptoms S, either he has or has not been vaccinated against Hypofluvia. If he hasn't, it is virtually certain that he has Hypofluvia; otherwise, Hypofluvia is counterindicated, but this is too unlikely a possibility to be considered seriously.

It seems to me that the intuition which was so sure in

Sect. I that Mrs. Duosmith doesn't really know her husband is dead is quite at a loss to say whether or not Dr. Pillsmith knows that Blotely has Hypofluvia. There is quicksand underfoot here, and we must not too hastily presume that Duosmith-type examples, which apparently refute the JTB analysis of knowledge by way of principle (A), are all that they seem to be.

III

It is now time to make explicit an important technical detail which is usually slighted in philosophical discussions of knowledge. This is that the judgmental attitudes in which a proposition can be held are not just belief and disbelief, or belief, disbelief, and uncertainty, but a whole spectrum of credibilities spanning many shades of uncertain belief and doubt. Consequently, assertion that knowing presupposes believing is specious unless it is made clear just how strong a belief is so required. Once this question of degree is raised, however, we can easily see from the absurdity of "He knows that p but isn't entirely sure of it,"[4] or "I know that p but have some doubts about whether it is really so," that only maximal belief is acceptable for knowledge. Hence condition (b) of the JTB thesis must be explicated as "X feels completely sure of p" or "X believes p absolutely," while similarly, (c) must be read as "X is justified in believing p absolutely," "X has a right to have not the slightest doubt about p," or the like. (Also, since it may be argued that if X is justified in believing p in degree d then X is also justified to almost the same extent in believing p to a degree which is almost d, "X is justified in believing p

---

[4] At first thought, this might seem to make sense as a variant of "He really knows that p but can't bring himself to admit it." But *not admitting to belief in* is not at all the same as *having some doubts about,* and "He knows that p but won't admit it" implies not "He is not sure of p and won't admit that p," but either "He doesn't really have any doubt about p but can't bring himself to say so," or "He still isn't really convinced of p even though he has overwhelming evidence for it."

absolutely" should be further explicated as "X has more justification for believing p absolutely than for feeling any doubt
about p.")

When is absolute belief justified? While a convincing general
answer is not easy to come by (see Sect. IV), a necessary condition for evidential justification is surely the following:

(B) If person X feels completely sure of p on the basis of
     evidence e, then X's belief in p is justified only if e
     necessitates p.

That is, X is not justified in feeling certain of p in virtue of his
awareness of e unless p is certain, given e. This is entirely
compatible with admitting that X may be justified in feeling
almost certain of p on grounds e if p is extremely likely, given
e. It only denies that it is rational for X to close his mind
completely to the possibility of not-p even though e, so long
as this possibility does in fact exist. Moreover, while (B) does
not specify what sense of necessity—logical, causal, or whatever—is required, it is in any case analytically true that

(C) If e while not q, then it is not the case that e necessi-
     tates q.

Finally, I think it will be agreed that in general,

(D) If person X feels completely sure of p only because he
     feels completely sure of q, but his belief in q is not
     justified, then neither is his belief in p justified.

(I would hold that (D) is always the case, but there is room
for argument on this point when q is "basic" for X (see Sect.
IV) and it is not essential here that (D) be completely universal.)

Let us now reconsider principle (A), which envisions a
person's believing p on the basis of his belief q, and q on the
basis of evidence e. For this to pose any threat to the JTB
analysis of knowledge, the degree of belief at issue must be

absolute belief. But it follows from (*B*) and (*C*) that *X* can justifiedly believe *q*—absolutely—on the basis of evidence *e* only if *q* is the case; so stipulation of *q*'s truth in the final clause of (*A*) is in this case otiose. That is, if *X* feels completely sure of *p* only because he is convinced of *q*, and the latter only because he is aware of *e*, then to hypothesize that *q* is false is also, by (*B*) and (*C*), to presuppose that *X*'s absolute belief in *q* is unjustified, and hence by (*D*) that neither is he justified in feeling completely sure of *p*. Thus in our Duosmith example (and similarly for Gettier's cases), while Mrs. Duosmith had excellent reason to feel *virtually* certain that her husband was dead, the bare fact that, overwhelming evidence to the contrary notwithstanding, the body before her was not that of her husband shows that this evidence did not warrant her having no doubt whatsoever that her husband was dead. Likewise, for our more problematic examples in Sect. II, we can say without hesitation that Mrs. Jones, Mr. Jones, and Dr. Pillsmith did not *know* that Mrs. Togethersmith was departing, that this board was less than 12 inches, and that Blotely had Hypofluvia, respectively, because while the evidential bases for these conclusions made them extremely likely, a vestige of uncertainty still remained. In short, if the "belief" cited in principle (*A*) is allowed to include degrees of belief weaker than complete conviction, the truth of (*A*) resides in that the falsity of *q* is symptomatic that the degree of *p*-belief justified by *e* is less than absolute.

IV

But while the argument from principle (*A*) thus fails to impeach the JTB thesis, the claim that justification is always prerequisite to knowledge is far from unproblematic. Most conspicuously troublesome is that if *X*'s knowing *p* requires there to exist evidence *e* such that *X*'s belief in *p* is justified by *X*'s awareness (i.e., knowledge) of *e*, then *X*'s belief in *e* also requires such justification and we are off on a regress. In particular, the justification requirement might seem to exclude the possibility of perceptual knowledge and self-awareness where

X's belief in p is not inferred from other beliefs but is aroused directly by sensory stimulation or given introspectively. Moreover, as will be seen, the demand for justification undergoes a remarkable transformation when we turn from other-person to first-person knowledge, while the conditions of justification even for the inferred beliefs of others are not so straightforward as they might at first appear.

Actually, no puzzle of "justification" can even discredit the JTB thesis, for the simple reason that whatever is needed for X to know that p, if X does know p then he is certainly justified in believing p. (Witness, e.g., the absurdity of "X knows that p, but he has no right to believe it so strongly.") So we can maintain that X knows that p iff p is a justified true belief of X's without concern for how murky the concept of justification may itself be. I submit, therefore, that the greatest philosophic challenge which issues from the JTB position is not to settle whether this view is entirely correct (though the import of my argument in Sect. III is that we have no good reason to doubt this), but to determine what it is about X's knowing p that accredits X's p-belief as "justified." The intent of this section is to rough out a tentative solution to this problem, which is more untidily complex than heretofore recognized, in full expectation that many more exchanges will be needed to round out the present survey in convincing detail.

Let a person's belief in p be described as "basic" if he does not believe p as a result of his believing something else. (For example, when X perceives that p, his belief in p is simply for him a *given* which becomes a basis for inference but is not derived from anything else he knows.) Then X's *basic convictions* are beliefs of which X feels completely sure without having inferred them from evidence. Unless knowledge can be inferred from beliefs which do not themselves qualify as knowledge (a counterintuitive possibility which I shall not discuss), the regression argument shows that if X knows anything at all, he must also have basic knowledge, i.e. justified true basic convictions, and our first task in this section is to find some acceptable sense in which a basic conviction may be said to be justified. Two alternatives present themselves:

either (1) basic convictions are self-justifying, or (2) some basic convictions have nonevidential justification.

In support of (1), it might be argued that the justification of X's belief in p consists in p's bearing a certain relation J to some set B of X's true basic convictions. If J is such that each $b_i \in B$ is also related to B in manner J, then all basic convictions in B are also by definition justified. For example, if "X is justified in believing p" were to be analyzed as "p is logically entailed by X's true basic convictions," then X's basic convictions are justified by the reflexivity of entailment. But this approach leaves much to be desired. For one, an intuitively acceptable J-relation with the needed formal properties is not easy to come by. (It is simple to argue, e.g., that logical entailment does not in itself confer evidential justification.) Further, how is the set B to be circumscribed? Does veracity suffice for a basic conviction to belong to B—i.e., for it to be justified? If so, we should have to grant that a dogmatic thinker who habitually works himself into a state of absolutely closed judgment on controversial issues without considering any of the relevant evidence is justified in holding any such belief which by chance happens to be true. But if we hold that a basic conviction can be true without necessarily being justified, whatever else is needed for the latter constitutes a nonevidential source of justification and thus carries us into alternative (2).

There are many intriguing thought experiments by which our intuitions about nonevidential belief-warrants can be bared, starting with increasingly bizarre or futuristic ways (e.g., electrical stimulation of the retina) in which sensory input might elicit true perceptual beliefs; but here it will suffice to consider just one which cuts directly to the heart of the matter. Suppose that Tom Seersmith claims to be able to foretell the outcomes of horse races. Upon investigation, we learn that when Seersmith thinks about a forthcoming race, he is often overwhelmed, quite without any reason for it, with a feeling of complete certainty that a certain horse will be the winner. Before the last Kentucky Derby, Seersmith felt sure that it would be won by a horse named Fleetfoot, and as it turned out his prediction was correct. Did Seersmith *know* that Fleetfoot was going to win, and if so, in what sense was his belief justified?

Whatever the personal peculiarity which endows Seersmith with convictions about forthcoming horse races, if his prognostication record has shown only chance accuracy in the past, we would be loath to say that Seersmith either knew or was justified in believing that Fleetfoot would win the Derby even though his belief in this instance happened to be true. Even if Seersmith's previous race predictions have usually been correct, with a hit rate high enough to convince us that there is something extraordinary about this man, we would still deny that he was justified in feeling absolutely sure that Fleetfoot would win so long as his predictions are not infallible. But suppose we discover that Seersmith's horse race prognoses *are* infallible—i.e., we become convinced that whenever Seersmith feels sure that race r will be won by horse h, it is absolutely certain that h will win r. Then surely we would be forced to admit that Seersmith knew that Fleetfoot would win the Derby, even though how he knew would baffle us. (As I follow Seersmith through prediction after prediction and see that he is *never* wrong, I find myself saying, "I can't understand it, but somehow, he *knows!*") The justification—nonevidential—for Seersmith's belief is simply that since generalization

$(\forall h)\ (\forall r)$ (Tom Seersmith believes that horse h will win race $r \supset h$ wins r)

is a nomological principle of our world, Seersmith's basic conviction that Fleetfoot would win the Derby was true not by mere happenstance but of nomic necessity. For if Seersmith's horse race precognitions *cannot* be wrong, what better justification could there possibly be for his having them?

Now let's change the case slightly. Tom Seersmith's brother Dick also feels occasional convictions about the outcomes of forthcoming horse races, but unlike his brother, Dick's percentage of correct anticipations is substantially less than perfect. Careful research discloses, however, that Dick's accuracy depends critically upon the horse's name. Whenever Dick feels sure that horse h will win race r, he is never mistaken so long as h's name contains exactly two syllables, but when the predicted winner's name is shorter or longer than this, Dick's precognitive effectiveness is somehow impaired. Dick, too, felt sure that Fleetfoot would win the Derby—but did he *know* this? In principle, Dick's case is exactly like that of brother Tom, since by natural law his preconvictions about bi-syllabically designated horse-race victors cannot err. Yet intuition is more hesitant here, for at times Dick also feels certain that h will win r when he should not, namely, when 'h' is not bi-syllabic. And if Dick is unaware that the anticipated winner's name makes a difference for the reliability of his forecast, we might question whether he is entitled to feel such perfect confidence in his precognition even when, unknown to him, it is in fact nomologically infallible. Thus it might be denied that Dick *knew* of Fleetfoot's forthcoming victory if he did not recognize that this particular belief had stronger truth-credentials than his average forecast. But this line of argument is unsound. If Dick were aware of his general precognitive fallibility, it would indeed seem reasonable for him to have inferential meta-doubts about his belief in Fleetfoot's victory— if he had, in fact, had any. But to make a person's knowing p contingent upon his knowing that he knows p would precipitate an intolerable regress, nor should a person's true belief in p be disqualified as knowledge merely by his having additional erroneous convictions as well. (To hold that a person can know nothing if he ever believes falsely seems extreme to the point of absurdity, though as will be seen in Sect. V it contains an important grain of truth.) If Dick's conviction that Fleetfoot would win the Derby was truly basic for him, uninfluenced by any meta-beliefs concerning his general prognostic proficiency, then it was for him no less an instance of *knowing* than it was for brother Tom, and was justified on the very same grounds, namely, that insomuch as Dick felt certain Fleetfoot would win, it *was* certain that Fleetfoot would win.

And now one more twist. Suppose that Harry is still another Seersmith whose case is like Dick's except that Harry's precognitions of form "horse h will win race r" are always (nomo-

logically) correct when and only when r is run on a dry
track. Insomuch as Fleetfoot won the Derby on a dry track,
was Harry's conviction that Fleetfoot would win an instance
of knowledge? Harry's belief, too, was infallible in that there
exists a nomic principle in virtue of which, given that Harry
felt sure that Fleetfoot would win and that the track was dry,
it was certain that Fleetfoot would win. But Harry differs from
Dick in that Dick's infallible precognitions are intrinsically
identifiable as such—i.e., whether or not a forecast by Dick
falls under the law which vouchsafes its accuracy is revealed
by its syllabic composition—whereas the reliability of Harry's
forecast cannot be determined without additional information
which does not generally become available until race time.
And since Harry thus cannot discriminate his infallible precognitions from those which are not (assuming that he does
not also have advance knowledge of the track conditions), it
might be argued that he had no right to feel so sure that Fleetfoot would win the Derby. But this doubt is only a refinement
of the one we have already rejected in Dick's case. If it is not
necessary for Harry to know that he knows p, or to know
that he can trust his belief p absolutely, in order for him to
know p or for his p-belief to be justified, then neither can we
reasonably hold that his being *able* to acquire this meta-
knowledge is requisite for the latter. (How could such an
ability possibly be germane except by way of the knowledge
which, with its help, Harry does acquire?) Consequently, so
long as a person's basic believing of p belongs to a class whose
members are nomologically infallible, its epistemological status
should not depend upon whether or not this class is defined
by properties inherent in the belief itself. (It is relevant to this
point that knowing what *we* know about Harry, we could win
a pretty penny at the races by noting Harry's prediction and
waiting to see the track conditions before deciding whether
to bet.)

The principle which appears to govern our Seersmith examples (though intuition speaks only with a subdued and
halting voice here) is that a basic conviction counts as "knowledge," and is by the same token justified, if and only if it not

merely *is* true, as could occur by chance, but is infallibly true by virtue of its being of a kind (perhaps defined in part by relational attributes) whose accuracy is guaranteed by natural law. This is at best an uneasy conclusion, however, for without further qualification it trembles on the brink of triviality: If V is the attribute of veridicality, then any belief of type V—i.e., any which happens to be true—is also infallibly true vis-à-vis type V and hence qualifies as knowledge unless "natural law" is defined to exclude generalizations which are logical truths. (That we would *like* to make some such exclusion is, I think, intuitively evident, but how to accomplish it effectively is another question.) Moreover, this criterion applies only to the basic convictions of other persons, for *my* beliefs, basic or otherwise, are justified by standards rather different from this.

Suppose that I set out to determine which of us, you or I, knows the more. I start by listing all propositions which you believe (or more precisely, all which I believe that you believe) and then prune this list by deleting everything on it which, in my judgment, is either false or is unwarranted for you. To display what *I* know, however (or rather, what I believe that I know), I list all the propositions believed by me —*and stop*. For while I am perfectly willing to admit that there are facts of which I have no knowledge, I do not believe, nor can I bring myself to believe, any specific proposition of form "*p*, but I don't know that *p*." This is closely related to the oddity of "*p*, but I don't believe it," but has a significance the latter does not. I reject "*p*, but I don't believe it" because my believing this would entail my believing *p* and hence falsify the conjunction as a whole—i.e., it is impossible for me to believe a true proposition of this form. I could, however, truly believe "*p*, but I don't know it" were *p* to be the case while I believed but did not know that *p*.[5] Hence my refusal to admit,

---

[5] While Hintikka [5] has proposed essentially the same analysis of "*p*, but I don't believe it" as offered here, his modal system allows that a person *can* defensibly claim to believe "*p*, but I don't know it." However, Hintikka's intuitive apologia for this [5, p. 83] construes it to involve a degree of *p*-belief less than perfect conviction, and the fact that his system does not recognize the unacceptability of "I don't know that

when I am convinced of p, that I may not know that p, has the force of maintaining that in *my* case, believing truly suffices for knowing. (And yet, when I reflect upon why I don't consider all *your* true beliefs to be knowledge, I am also willing to admit in general terms that some of mine may not be knowledge, either. This is an apparent inconsistency which will be resolved in Sect. V.)

This first-person/other-person difference in knowledge criteria is present even when, from your vantage point, my true belief is amply justified. Suppose that I believe mathematical theorem T because I have just discovered a convincing proof of it, and when I inform you that I know T, you ask me what grounds I have for thinking that I know this. The only reply which seems relevant is for me to recapitulate the steps by which I deduced T—except that when I do this, you quite properly point out that what I have given you is grounds for believing T whereas what you asked for is grounds for believing that I know T. My supplying of proof for T *demonstrates* to you that my belief in T is justified, but *asserts* nothing which implies this. On the other hand, if I try to give you an account of how it is that I know T, it will go something like: "Well, I know that L_1 and L_2 are logically true, so when I see that T is an immediate consequence of L_1 and L_2, this makes me aware that T is also the case." What I am telling you is that my awareness of certain facts, namely, that L_1 and L_2 are logically true and jointly entail T, is a *cause* of my knowing T. But from your perspective, my awareness of this evidence *provides* (noncausally, by fulfilling an existence requirement) the justification which is an analytic component of my knowing T. That is, in more general terms, when I have come to know p by a valid line of reasoning from unimpeachable premises, the inferential procedure which to you is a *condition* on my knowing p is to me only the *occasion* for this. What justifies *my* believing p is simply p's being the case; for once I have convinced myself that p, I require nothing else to con-

---

p even though I am absolutely sure of it" would seem to reveal a lacuna in its axioms.

sider it right that I feel sure of p—what more could possibly be relevant? In fact, it is nomically impossible for me to accept "p, but I have no right to believe it so absolutely," for my believing the second component of this suffices to create some doubt in me about p. (This is why I am unable—nomically, not logically—to believe "p, but I don't know it.") So I reason about p not to transmute my base belief in p into golden knowledge, but to decide whether p is the case; whereupon, having convinced myself that it is, I rebuff all challenges to my conviction's epistemic credentials by the argument "p; therefore it is reasonable for me to believe that p."

What are my criteria for the justification of *your* beliefs? We have already explored the evaluation of your basic convictions, but it remains to see what is needed for your inferred beliefs to be reasonable. Ordinarily, the degree of p-belief which I consider evidence e to warrant in you is simply the confidence in p which I sense is aroused in me by conviction that e. However, closer analysis shows this not to be definitive. Let p and q be two propositions such that q logically entails p. If, somehow, I know that you know q, what will persuade me that you have evidential justification for believing p? For myself, merely being cognizant of q does not in itself convince me of p (I am, after all, often unsure of consequences of my beliefs when I have not discerned that they are such consequences), so for your q-awareness to warrant your p-belief, I would normally require you to know not only that q, but that q entails p as well. But is q & ($q \vdash p$) then *sufficient* evidence to justify your belief in p? If, either thoughtlessly or with good reason, I presume that our minds work alike, I will agree that it is; for belief in the former would cause me to believe the latter as well. But suppose I have learned that you just don't seem to grasp the significance of logical relationships; specifically, that you often accept propositions of form "α, and α entails β" while simultaneously doubting or even disbelieving β. Then I would no longer consider your belief in q & ($q \vdash p$) to be evidential justification for your believing p, for I could not regard the former as the *source* of the latter, nor would I have reason to regard your p-belief as knowledge insomuch as your veridicality in this instance may simply be the chance success of irrational thought. Conversely suppose I discover instead that your thinking is superrational in that for any two propositions α and β such that α entails β, and you believe α, your mere thinking of β when you believe α suffices for you to be convinced of β as well—i.e., you believe all logical consequences of your beliefs, so long as they come to mind at all, whether or not you are also aware of the entailment relations among these propositions. In this case, I must concede that your knowledge of q is fully adequate in itself to justify, and hence to dignify as knowledge, your belief in p. For if you accept all logical consequences of your convictions, rather than just a proper subclass of these constrained by your logistical perceptiveness, on what grounds can I hold your belief processes to be epistemically defective?

The preceding arguments show, first impressions to the contrary notwithstanding, that my other-person epistemology has exactly the same justificational standards for inferred beliefs as it does for basic ones. In both cases, the critical determinant is not whether the belief in question is "reasonable" in accord with some impersonal normative ideal, but whether it has arisen in circumstances which guarantee its accuracy. (This applies also to beliefs with derivational status intermediate between basic and inferred, thus bypassing the problems these would generate were the criteria of justification qualitatively different for the two extremes. For example, suppose that for a certain pair of attributes P and Q, whenever you perceive that $P(a)$ for an object a you find yourself also convinced that $Q(a)$. If I know that in our world P nomically implies Q, I must count your belief in $Q(a)$ as knowledge, justified by your awareness of $P(a)$, even if you are not consciously aware that $(\forall x)[P(x) \supset Q(x)]$.)[6] Harmony between

---

[6] I say "not consciously aware" rather than simply "unaware" to suggest the glide from inference episodes of the most paradigmatically rational sort down to believings which are patterned *as though* they were accompanied by additional supportive knowledge which the believer does not, in fact, have in any conceptualized form.

first-person and other-person justification, however, is more elusive. At one level, these show a common pattern: Whenever I consider my/your conviction in p to be justified, I presume there to exist an argument of form "S; hence my/your belief in p is necessarily correct," where S is some state of reality.[7] But when it is my belief which is at issue, S is p itself; whereas I want the S which warrants your p-belief to do so nomically rather than logically. That I should adopt so flagrant an epistemological double standard is not a conclusion which I find esthetically pleasing, but if there is a deeper unity here I have yet to find it.

V

However lacking in clarity (and perhaps consistency) the epistemic concept of "justification" may be, it nonetheless appears that knowing p analytically requires not only that the knower feel completely certain of p, but also that there be some sense in which, considering the circumstances, it *is* completely certain that p. But since I reject the argument "p; therefore you are justified in feeling sure of p," and also doubt that our *de facto* world contains any nomic regularities perfect enough to vouchsafe any belief beyond all possibility of error, I do not think that you strictly know anything at all. Whereas in my own case, I have too much faith in my own fallibility to feel *absolutely* sure of anything, even if some of my perceptual beliefs fall short of this only negligibly. My admission (with high but not complete conviction) that probably not all of my beliefs are entirely correct, plus inability to meta-distinguish those which are true from those which are not, causally prevents me from ever entirely achieving an absolute extremity of belief, while my professioinal skills as scientist and philosopher enable me to find genuine even if minuscule

[7] The scope of "necessary" here is of course $N(S \supset$ my-or-your p-belief is correct), not $S \supset N$ (my-or-your p-belief is correct).

chinks of uncertainty in any proposition I examine, even those which arise perceptually or feel analytically true. So technically speaking, I know nothing either.[8]

In short, my conception of "knowledge"—and presumably yours as well—is so impossibly idealized that no real-life belief episode ever satisfies it. Whenever you or I assert, as we often do, "I am aware that . . ." "He knows that . . ." etc., we are uttering falsehoods which would come closer to the truth if revised as "I approximate awareness that . . ." "He almost knows that . . ." or the like. The paradigm-case rejoinder, that what we *mean* by "know" is defined by these ordinary-life applications, no more shows that this usage is literally correct than the everyday paradigmatic ascriptions of "spherical" to roundish objects of irregular curvature demonstrates that a thing's surface does not really have to be a constant distance from its center in order for it to be literally a sphere. On matters philosophical as well as scientific, ordinary language teems with simplistic presuppositions and coarse-grained, uncritical categories which do slovenly justice to reality; and intellectual maturity—represented most illustriously by technical science but by no means restricted thereto—consists first of all in learning to relinquish these cognitive crudities for a more sophisticated grasp of complexity and precise detail. It is all very well to recognize that the conceptual fluency of idealized approximations is often more convenient for everyday affairs than is the encumbrance of needless exactitude, but it is folly to construe the success of this practical usage as a sign that what is so asserted is precisely correct, or to begrudge its abandonment when, like outgrown clothing, its inaccuracies begin to chafe. In particular, there is no more reason for us to agonize philosophically over the esoterics of everyday knowledge-talk —e.g., why justified true beliefs at practical levels of assurance should sometimes be called knowledge and sometimes not— than for geometricians to puzzle over why some common-sense

---

[8] Hence the title of this paper is something of a misnomer. Although my knowledge criteria are enormously more liberal for me than for you, their extension is in both cases the null class.

spheres have a larger cubed-surface-to-squared-volume ratio than do others.

To conclude, then, I propose that the subject of "knowledge" is no longer of serious philosophical concern for the simple reason that this concept is far too primitive for the needs of technical epistemology. No harm will be done, I suppose, by retaining a special name for true beliefs at the theoretical limit of absolute conviction and perfect infallibility so long as we appreciate that this ideal is never instantiated, but such sentimentality must not be allowed to impede development of conceptual resources for mastering the panorama of partial certainties which are more literally relevant to the real world. So far, however, the normative theory of practical belief has scarcely advanced beyond surmise that the structure of propositional credibilities is isomorphic to the probability calculus, and has not even begun to think technically about such vital subtleties as the ramifications of uncertainty in basic beliefs, reciprocal nondemonstrative supports among partially confirmed propositions, the credibility interplay between beliefs and meta-beliefs, and the like. With problems of "How strongly should X believe p?" lying dark and unfathomed before us, we stand to profit from continued epistemological preoccupation with the nature of "knowledge" to just about the same extent as would psychology from a return to study of the "soul."

PART THREE

DOES KNOWING IMPLY BELIEVING?

Jonathan Harrison

Does Knowing Imply Believing?

I

Concerning the relation of knowing to believing, two views
have commonly been held. According to the first, belief is implied by knowledge: if Jones knows he has cancer, then Jones
must, among other things, believe that he has cancer. Probably
he must not, on this view, merely believe this, but believe it
very strongly, perhaps to the extent of being certain, or even
absolutely certain, that he has cancer, and, of course, that he
has cancer must be true. According to the second, knowledge,
so far from implying belief, excludes it. If Jones knows he has
cancer, he cannot just believe that he has; and if he just believes he has cancer, he cannot possibly know that he has. According to the first view, belief is a necessary, but not a
sufficient, condition of knowledge; if Jones does not even believe, then Jones cannot know. According to the second view,
believing is a sufficient condition of not knowing; if Jones *does*
believe, then Jones cannot know.

I believe that there is something to be said in favour of each
of these two views. In favour of the second we can say this. If
I were to say 'I believe my name is Harrison', I should be talking oddly, for this is something I would normally be prepared
to say I knew. And if I were to say of Mr. Macmillan 'He believes that he is Prime Minister' I should, again, be talking

From *The Philosophical Quarterly*, 13 (1963), 322–332. Reprinted by
permission of the author and *The Philosophical Quarterly*.

very oddly, because this is something I would normally be prepared to say that Mr. Macmillan knew. 'He believes he is Prime Minister' is a statement we should normally make about patients in mental hospitals.

In favour of the first view, however, it can be said that being quite sure, alas, feels just like knowing, and the knower or believer cannot by introspection tell which is which. Furthermore, we behave with regard to the propositions we are certain of just as we behave with regard to the propositions we know. We will bet just as much on what we are certain of as we will on what we know, and shout just as loudly if we are contradicted. Hence there must be an emotional and/or behavioural core, which knowing and believing have in common. He who knows, as well as he who believes, must believe, though, over and above this, he who knows is right, and has, perhaps, established the truth of what he knows by the proper application of some accredited method.

This argument in favour of the view that knowing implies believing seems to me to be very strong. Why, then, if our first view is correct, is it improper to say 'I believe my name is Harrison' or 'Mr. Macmillan believes he is Prime Minister' when, if knowing implies believing, and we do know these things, that we believe them must be true?

II

To answer this question, recourse must be had to a distinction between what a sentence enables one to assert about its subject matter, and what its use would naturally tend to cause anyone hearing it to infer about the person writing or uttering it. One example of this distinction is already well known. Though the sentence 'It is raining' is not about me, but about the weather, anyone hearing me say 'It is raining' is entitled to infer that I believe it is raining. That I believe it is raining is not something I say; nor is it a necessary condition of the truth of what I say, for, if I say 'It is raining', it may so happen that what I say is true, even though I am saying something I do not believe. Though 'It is raining' is not necessarily false when it is uttered by someone who does not believe that it is raining, he is acting improperly in saying it. Even if it does not mislead the hearer about the weather, it is calculated to mislead the hearer about the speaker, i.e., to make the hearer think the speaker believes something which he does not. His saying it is improper, even though what he says is not necessarily false. His saying 'It is raining' evinces, shows, demonstrates or manifests that he believes it is raining, even though 'It is raining' does not logically imply that the speaker believes it is raining. It is, furthermore, for an excellent reason that we do not allow people to say things they do not believe, for, when they do, they are very unlikely to say what is true.

Perhaps this distinction,[1] between the falsity of a proposition and the impropriety of uttering it because of what it shows about the state of mind of the speaker, will help us to explain why we should not say things like 'Mr. Macmillan believes he is Prime Minister' and 'I believe my name is Harrison', even though—as they will be if knowing implies believing—these things are true.

III

That use has to be made of this distinction is shown when we consider the relation between propositions of the form 'X knows p' and propositions asserted by the sentence 'I know p', when this sentence is asserted by the person who says 'X knows p'. Someone hearing me say 'Jones knows that he has cancer' will be entitled to complain if I refuse to say 'I know Jones has cancer'. My hearer will feel that I have been guilty of some impropriety, that I have misled him in some way, if I say that someone else knows that something is the case, and it turns out that, because I have not made up my own mind on the question whether this is the case or not, I would not say that *I* knew it was the case. In other words, I show that I think I know p by saying 'X knows p' just as much as I do by saying 'I know p', though only the latter statement has to be *false* in the event of my not knowing p.

---

[1] The reader is referred to the articles on the subject in *Philosophy and Analysis* (ed. Margaret Macdonald), Ch. IV.

That there is this impropriety in my saying that other people know things which I would not say that I myself knew, is further shown by the fact that there is something very wrong with the sentence 'Jones knows he has cancer, but I do not know whether he has cancer or not', and with the sentence 'Jones knows he has cancer, but I do not know he has cancer'. These sentences are peculiar in the same sort of way that 'It is raining, but I myself have no opinion on the question whether it is raining or not' or 'It is raining, but I do not believe that it is' are peculiar.

That 'Jones knows he has cancer, but I do not know whether he has cancer or not', or 'Jones knows he has cancer, but I do not know he has' are improper may be obscured by the fact that it is not at all improper to say 'Jones knows what is the matter with him, but I do not', or 'Jones knows the answer, but I do not'. Other people, obviously, can know many things which I do not know, and, equally obviously, I may know that they do. When the word 'know' is followed by a word or phrase like 'the answer' or 'the date' or 'when . . .' or 'how . . .' or 'why . . .', which does not say precisely what the proposition known is, there is nothing improper in my saying 'Jones knows, but I do not'. The impropriety I am talking about only arises when the word 'know' is followed by a form of words, such as 'the unknown number is 3.3' or 'the Battle of Hastings was fought in 1066', which do specify what the proposition known is, and which could be used in other contexts to make a statement.

IV

Given that 'X knows p, but I do not' and 'p, but I do not believe p' are both improper, are they improper in the same sort of way? We have seen that anyone asserting p does not logically imply that he believes p. If he did, then propositions such as 'It is raining' or 'Pigs cannot fly' would be false when asserted by people who do not believe them. From the fact that 'Pigs cannot fly' does not logically imply that the speaker believes that they cannot, it follows that 'Pigs cannot fly, but I do not believe that they cannot' is not contradictory. What is wrong with 'Pigs cannot fly, but I do not believe that they cannot' is that 'Pigs cannot fly' evinces or manifests a belief which 'I do not believe that they cannot' explicitly denies. The impropriety involved is not the impropriety of saying something which is false, or of saying something which implies what is false, but the impropriety of saying something which evinces or demonstrates a belief which I do not in this case have.

The same is true of 'X knows p, but I do not'. If 'X knows p' logically implied that I knew p, then sentences of the form 'X knows p' would express something false when asserted by people who did not themselves know p. Whether such sentences expressed propositions which were true or false would depend upon who the person was who made them, for obviously whether 'I know p' expresses a truth or a falsehood will depend upon who says it, and so, if 'X knows p' logically implies that the person speaking must be able truly to say 'I know p', propositions such as 'X knows p' must depend for their truth or falsity upon who asserts them. Propositions like 'X knows p', however, do not depend for their truth or falsity upon who asserts them, and are not false when asserted by people who do not themselves know the truth of what they say others know. Just as I can say 'It is raining' when I do not believe that it is, and my statement, by chance, can turn out to be true, so I can say 'Jones knows he has cancer' when I do not know he has cancer, and my statement, by chance, can turn out to be true. Hence 'X knows p' does not logically imply 'I know p', and 'X knows p, but I do not' is not self-contradictory. When I say 'X knows p' I demonstrate or evince my own confidence in p, but I do not assert or logically imply that I know it. And when I say 'X knows p, but I do not' I do not contradict myself. I explicitly deny, in the second part of the sentence, that I have the attitude which is evinced in the first part.

V

The impropriety of 'p, but I do not believe p' arises in the following way. People generally say only what they believe.

If they do not say what they believe, there must be a reason
for it, and the most likely, though not the only, reason is that
they want to deceive someone else into thinking what is not
true. If they want to do this, however, they will defeat their
own ends if they say to the very same people at the very same
time that they do not believe it. If, on the other hand, the
villain in a melodrama says 'Nothing could be safer' and then
adds, *aside to the audience,* 'But I don't believe it', no impropriety, other than moral, is involved.

The reason for the impropriety of saying that someone else
knows p, though we do not, is different, I think, in two different types of situation in which sentences of the form 'X
knows p' are commonly used. Sometimes we say that someone
else knows something, when we ourselves already know that
thing, and are pronouncing, in a capacity resembling that of
judge or examiner, upon the question whether this other person knows this thing too. Now in one type of case an examiner
can perfectly well assess the merits of some performances without himself being able to do the things he is assessing. One can
judge a sheep-dog trial without being able to bark. Testing
other people's claims to know certain things, however, does not
fall within this category, and if I say that X knows p, I am myself claiming to be in a position to decide whether he really
does know or not, and thus claiming that I am in the only
situation in which I could properly do this—i.e., in the situation of one who knows these things himself. If I say 'X knows
p, but I do not', the impropriety involved, then, if the case is
one like this, is the impropriety of doing something which I
can do only if I am in a certain position, viz., one of knowing
p, and at the same time saying that I am not in this position.

The situation in which I judge someone else's claim to know
cannot be the only case in which I can say of someone else
that he knows something. If it were, I could never come to
know anything as a result of being told it by someone else who
knew it first, and passed on his knowledge to me, for, if I can
pronounce upon other people's claims to know things only in
the guise of an examiner, I must always know *first* what they
tell me they know, and so cannot add to my stock of knowl-

edge because of what they say. However, even in the case when knowledge is transmitted from someone else to me by my accepting his testimony or recognizing his authority, my deciding that he knows the truth of what he is telling me implies that I have now resolved any doubts I may previously have had about it; that I now think I too know it. For example, if my doctor tells me that unless I give up smoking I have only two more years to live, and I decide that he knows this and is not saying it just to encourage me to stop, I must also decide that, since I have been told this by someone who I admit knows, I now know this too. 'X knows p, but I do not' is improper because I should not say that X knows p while doubts concerning p linger on, and, if no doubts concerning p do linger, then I ought not to say that I do not know p.

It is not my view that if X knows p, and tells Y, Y must then know p. This is simply not the case. X, who witnessed the accident, may say in court that the driver failed to signal his intention of turning to the right, and know this, because he saw quite clearly what happened. Yet, if X is notoriously unreliable, the jury are quite justified in not placing much reliance on the truth of what he says. In this case, they clearly do not know that the driver failed to signal, even though they have been told by someone who did know. The erroneous view that if I have been told by someone who knows, I know, is quite different from the view I have been putting forward, that if I say that X knows p, I ought not to say that I do not.

VI

Here, I think, it is important to guard against a possible confusion. My saying 'X knows p' does not evince or demonstrate my *knowledge* that p. What it does evince is that I am prepared to *say* 'I know p'. That these two things are different is shown by the fact that I am prepared to say, and say quite sincerely, that I know many things which I do not in fact know. From this it follows that there is nothing improper, so far as what it evinces about myself goes, in my saying 'X knows p' when I do not know p, so long as I think I do, and am quite prepared, deception aside, to say that I do.

VII

My saying 'Jones knows p', therefore, shows, when used properly, that I am prepared to say 'I know p', and, though I am not necessarily saying something false when I say 'Jones knows p', but am not prepared to say 'I know p', I am using language in an improper way, and am liable to mislead my hearers about myself, even if it so happens that I do not mislead them about Jones. The next question is, what shall we say about 'Jones *believes* p'? Does this indicate anything about my confidence or otherwise in the proposition I say Jones believes?

It is apparent that by saying 'Jones believes' I avoid evincing a confidence in p which I would have evinced had I said 'Jones knows p'. But our problem was to explain why the person who could say 'Jones knows p' would be using language oddly if he said 'Jones believes p'; to explain, for example, why it is odd to say 'Mr. Macmillan believes he is Prime Minister' when I would be prepared to say that Mr. Macmillan knew that he was Prime Minister. Clearly, however, there is nothing wrong with failing to evince a confidence in p which I happen to have. For it to be wrong to say 'Mr. Macmillan believes he is Prime Minister' it must be the function of 'believe' not just to enable me not to evince confidence, but actually to evince lack of confidence—or, at any rate, lack of complete confidence. If 'X knows p' evinced confidence, and 'X believes p' evinced lack of confidence, then it would be improper for the same person to say both.

To the view that 'X believes p' evinces lack of confidence in p, that I say 'X believes p' rather than 'X knows p', because I am myself not prepared to say 'I know p', it may be objected that I may prefer to use the former expression for a number of other reasons. I may be perfectly prepared to say that I know p, but choose to say that Jones believes p, because I do not think he is sufficiently confident of the truth of p to be properly described as knowing it. I may be perfectly prepared to say that I know p, but refuse to say that Jones knows p, because I am not satisfied that Jones came to the conclusion that p for the right reasons. Jones may have been perfectly certain that his horse would win the Derby, and his horse may actually have won the Derby, and I may be prepared to say that I knew it won the Derby, but unprepared to say that Jones knew it would, because Jones's reason for thinking that it would was that its number was thirteen. Lastly, I may be perfectly prepared to say that I know p, and perfectly prepared to say that Jones knows p, but, nevertheless, say that Jones believes p simply because, in certain circumstances—perhaps because all that matters is Jones's attitude to p, and not whether p is true or not—I do not need to commit myself to more than is necessary.

These contentions may be true, though personally I am inclined to think that, given we ourselves think we know p, we are not as exacting in our demand that others should be firmly convinced of p, and for good reasons, as most philosophers seem to think. Fortunately, however, this is not a statement I need to substantiate here. For it seems fairly obvious that by far the most common reason for choosing to say 'X believes' rather than 'X knows' is that the speaker is not prepared to commit himself to saying that he knows p. Hence there is always a great danger that, when we say 'X believes p' when we *are* prepared to say that we know p, we will mislead our hearers into thinking that we think we do not know that p.

It must be reemphasized that whether our statement 'X believes p' is true or not has nothing to do with whether we ourselves are or are not prepared to say that we know p. If, improperly, we say 'X believes p', when we are prepared to say that we know p, then what is wrong with our statement is not that it is false, but that it evinces an attitude to p which we do not have, and so may cause our hearers to infer things about ourselves which are false.

VIII

There are, therefore, two things to be considered about statements to the effect that other people know or believe certain things, where the things which they are alleged to know or believe are fully stated, as in 'She knew that his horse would lose the race'. They may be true or false, depending upon whether the person spoken of does know or believe these things, and they may or may not be calculated to mislead people about the speaker, according as to whether they evince that he is or is not prepared to say that he knows or believes these things. Whether these statements are true or false is logically quite independent of whether or not they are misleading about the speaker. Set out systematically, the possible cases are these:

A1. Smith says 'Jones knows he has cancer'. Jones does know he has cancer. Smith has no doubt in his mind that Jones has cancer, and is quite prepared to say that he (Smith) knows Jones has cancer. In this case, Smith is both making a true statement about Jones, and is not misleading anyone about himself by indicating that he thinks he knows when he does not think he knows.

A2. Smith says 'Jones knows he has cancer'. Jones does know he has cancer. Smith, however, would not be prepared to say he knew Jones had cancer. In this case, what Smith says is still true, but will be misleading about Smith, because it evinces a readiness on Smith's part to say 'I know Jones has cancer' which Smith does not have.

A3. Smith says 'Jones knows he has cancer'. It is false that Jones knows he has cancer. (I say 'It is false that Jones knows he has cancer' rather than 'Jones does not know he has cancer', because the latter suggests 'Jones has cancer, but is not aware that he has', which is not the strict contradictory of 'Jones knows he has cancer'.) Smith, however, does think he knows, and can sincerely say that he knows, that Jones has cancer. In this case, Smith's statement, though false, does not mislead by evincing an attitude which Jones does not have.

A4. Smith says 'Jones knows he has cancer'. It is false that Jones knows he has cancer. Smith is also not prepared to say that he knows that Jones has cancer. In this case, Smith's statement is both false and calculated to mislead by evincing an attitude which Smith does not have.

B1. Smith says 'Jones believes he has cancer'. Jones does believe he has cancer. (The preceding sentence is an interesting case of an occasion when it is possible to say 'Jones believes' without evincing either a preparedness or an unpreparedness to say 'I know p' on the part of the person—in this case myself—using the expression.) Smith would not be prepared to say that he knew Jones had cancer. In this case, what Smith says is both true about Jones, and not misleading about Smith.

B2. Smith says 'Jones believes he has cancer'. Jones does believe he has cancer. Smith, however, would be prepared to say that he knew Jones had cancer. In this case, what Smith says is true, but would tend to mislead people about Smith, since it may evince an unpreparedness on Smith's part to say that he knows Jones has cancer.

B3. Smith says 'Jones believes he has cancer'. Jones does not believe he has cancer. Smith, too, would not be prepared to say that he knew Jones had cancer. In this case, what Smith says is false, but it will not mislead anyone about Smith.

B4. Smith says 'Jones believes he has cancer'. Jones does not believe he has cancer. Smith, however, thinks he knows Jones has cancer, and would be prepared to say 'I know Jones has cancer'. In this case, what Smith says both is false about Jones, and tends to mislead about Smith, for it may evince an unpreparedness to say 'I know Jones has cancer' when Jones is prepared to say this.

IX

If what has been said is correct, it is now possible to see what is right and what wrong both with the claim that knowing implies believing, and with the claim that knowing excludes believing, in so far as these claims apply to knowledge or belief statements about other people. If we distinguish between conditions for the truth of statements about what other people know or believe, and conditions for their propriety, for their evincing an attitude on the part of the speaker, or for their tending or not tending to mislead others about the speaker, it is possible to see that the claim that knowing implies believing is right in so far as it applies to the truth of such statements, whereas the claim that knowing excludes believing is right in so far as it applies to their evincing the speaker's attitude. The claim that knowing excludes believing is correct in that someone who thinks he knows p should generally not say 'X believes p', and, except in certain circumstances, cannot do so without misleading people into thinking that he would not himself be prepared to claim that he knows p. This claim is correct, too, to the extent that someone who is not prepared to say that he knows p (i.e. who thinks that he does not know p) cannot say 'X knows p' without misleading people into thinking that he is prepared to say that he knows p. In other words, if he can say 'X knows p' without misleading other people about himself, he usually cannot say 'X believes p' without misleading other people about himself, and vice versa. But though the propriety of 'X knows p' generally excludes the propriety of 'X believes p', and vice versa, this does not at all mean that the truth of 'X knows p' does not imply the truth of 'X believes p'. The truth of 'X knows p' does imply the truth of 'X believes p'. The trouble is that the person who can properly say 'X knows p' usually cannot properly say 'X believes p', for one or the other of these two expressions will, generally, tend to mislead his hearers about himself.

That the truth of 'X knows p' implies the truth of 'X believes p' can be seen more clearly if we introduce to Jones and Smith a third person, Robinson. Let us suppose that Jones knows that he has cancer, and has given clear indication that he believes he has both to Smith and Robinson, but that, whereas Smith thinks he knows that Jones's belief is true, i.e., thinks he knows that Jones has cancer, Robinson has no opinion on the question of the truth of Jones's belief. In this case, if Smith says 'Jones knows he has cancer' his remark is quite in order; it will be both true about Jones, and will not evince an attitude which Smith does not have, or tend to mislead anyone about him. If Robinson says 'Jones knows he has cancer', however, though what he says will be true about Jones, it will tend to mislead people about Robinson; to mislead them into thinking that Robinson thinks he knows that Jones has cancer, for this is what Robinson's saying 'Jones knows p' evinces. What Robinson ought to say, of course, is 'Jones believes he has cancer', and, if he says this, it will both be true about Jones, and not misleading about Robinson. If, however, Smith were to say 'Jones believes he has cancer', this would tend to mislead people about Smith—to mislead people into thinking that Smith would not be prepared to say that he knew that Jones had cancer. If we are not to adopt the extraordinary view, already rejected, that statements about what other people believe are relative, in the sense that their truth depends upon the person who makes them, we must allow that if Robinson had said 'Jones knows he has cancer' he would have been saying something true (because this was true when Smith said it), and that if Smith had said 'Jones believes he has cancer', he also would have been saying something true (because this was true when Robinson said it). From this it follows that 'Jones knows he has cancer', said by either Smith or Robinson, implies 'Jones believes he has cancer', said by either Smith or Robinson—or, for that matter, said by anybody. For if Smith's assertion 'Jones knows he has cancer' is in order, it follows that Robinson's assertion 'Jones believes he has cancer' is in order, and from this it follows that, since the truth of statements of the form 'X believes p' does not depend upon who makes them, if Smith had said 'Jones believes he has cancer', his assertion—though not entirely in order, for Smith thinks he knows Jones has cancer—is, at any rate, true.

X

So far, I have only talked about the conditions of the truth, and the conditions for the propriety, of statements about what other people know and believe. Can the above remarks be extended to explain why the person who is prepared to say, in the first person, 'I know . . .', is, and should be, reluctant to say 'I believe . . .', and why the person who is prepared to say, in the first person, 'I believe . . .', is, and should be, reluctant to say 'I know . . .'? Can we say that if 'I know p' is true, then 'I believe p' must be true too, though if 'I know p' is not misleading about the speaker—because he does think he knows, which is what 'I know p' evinces—'I believe p' will be misleading about the speaker, and vice versa?

It is obvious that there is a difference, which is, on the face of it, important, between the case of 'He knows . . .' and 'He believes . . .' on the one hand, and the case of 'I know . . .' and 'I believe . . .' on the other. In the former case, the person about whom knowledge or belief statements are true or false is a different person from the person—i.e., the speaker, in both cases—about whom they are or are not misleading. In the latter case, however, the person about whom they are true or false is the same as the person about whom they are or are not misleading, for the speaker is talking about himself. This might lead one to suppose that the question whether knowledge or belief statements are true, and the question whether they evince an attitude which the speaker does or does not have, cannot be distinguished when these statements are in the first person. If X knows, and says 'I know . . .' then, if what he says is true, it cannot be misleading, and if what he says is not misleading, it must be true. This, however, is a mistake. It has already been pointed out that what knowledge or belief statements evince about the speaker is not his knowledge or belief, but his preparedness or unpreparedness, deception apart, to say 'I know . . .' or to refuse to say this. From this it follows that whether his remark 'I know . . .' is true or not will depend upon whether or not he does know, but whether or not his remark is misleading will depend upon whether or not he thinks he knows. If, for example, he says he knows when he doesn't know, but thinks he does, what he says is false, but it will not be misleading. If, on the other hand, he says 'I believe . . .' when he does not know, but thinks he does, what he says will be misleading though it will not be false.

Let us suppose that Jones both knows, and is aware that he knows, that he has cancer. Let us suppose that Smith also knows Jones has cancer, and says 'Jones knows he has cancer'. Let us suppose that Robinson does not know whether Jones has cancer or not, and says 'Jones believes he has cancer'. I have argued that what both Smith and Robinson say is true, and that neither is misleading about either speaker. It seems to me that from the fact that Smith can truly say 'Jones knows he has cancer', it follows that Jones can truly say 'I know I have cancer'; and it seems to me to follow from the fact that Robinson can truly say 'Jones believes he has cancer', that Jones can truly say 'I believe I have cancer'. Hence, if Jones does say 'I believe I have cancer', what he says is perfectly true (its truth, indeed, follows from the truth of what Jones says when he says 'I know I have cancer'). What will be wrong with it is that it will tend to mislead anyone hearing Jones say it into thinking that Jones would not be prepared to say that he knew he had cancer, for 'I believe I have cancer' normally evinces an unwillingness to say 'I know I have cancer'.

Hence there is no reason why the views put forward above about the relation between 'He knows . . .' and 'He believes . . .' should not apply also to the relation between 'I know . . .' and 'I believe . . .'. It would be tedious to set out a systematic schema for all the possible cases, in the manner in which I have already done it for 'He knows . . .' and 'He believes . . .'. It is worth noting, however, that there are, where 'I know . . .' and 'I believe . . .' are concerned, two anomalous cases. The case which arises if you suppose Smith to be talking about himself instead of Jones in A2 above, is *perhaps* impossible, for it implies the possibility of knowing something without knowing that one knows it, which some philosophers would maintain to be impossible. And the case which arises if you make the same alteration to B4 above, is *certainly* not possible, for it is clearly impossible for anyone to think he knows something, when he does not even believe it.

XI

My conclusion is that knowing does imply believing, and that the view that these exclude one another is a misinterpretation of the fact that the person who can properly say 'X knows p' or 'I know p' cannot, as a general rule, properly say 'X believes p' or 'I believe p'.

Even this, it must be remembered, is not always true. There are probably occasions—though, if there are, I think they are rarer than most philosophers believe—when we cannot say of someone else that he knows what we know, because, though he does believe it, he does not believe it strongly enough, or there is something wrong with the way in which he arrived at this belief. And there are occasions when we can say 'X thinks . . .' or 'I think . . .' not only without committing ourselves to being prepared to say that we know, which 'think' or 'believe' always enables us to do, but without even evincing an unpreparedness to say we know. If there were no way of talking about peoples' opinions without evincing one's own attitude to their rationality or truth, it would be necessary to invent one. There are times when we are interested solely in the strength of other people's beliefs,[2] in the way in which they manifest themselves, in their distribution, their correlation with, say, the social class of their owners, or their malleability, rather than in their justification and truth, and in such cases we shall naturally wish to talk about them without irrelevantly giving away our own attitude to them, which attitude it is, sometimes inconveniently, generally one of the functions of the word 'believes' to show.

[2] It is interesting that when we talk about a person's *beliefs,* we evince no attitude to their rationality or truth; among a person's beliefs are the things he knows, as well as the things he is irrationally convinced of and the things he is wrong about. This is perhaps because there is, in English, no word which stands to 'knows' in the relation which 'belief' stands in to 'believes', and so the one word 'belief' has to do duty for both.

Colin Radford

Knowledge—By Examples

Example 1

MAN: Look, I *know* I locked the car. Still—I'll go back and make
absolutely sure.

WIFE (*irritated*): Aren't you sure?

MAN: Well—*yes*, I *am* sure. I'd bet money on it. Still, I could be
mistaken. It's possible, isn't it darling? And this is a tough
neighborhood.

WIFE (*surprised*): Oh!

MAN: Yes. And since it would be disastrous if I hadn't locked it, I
might as well go and check. I won't be long.

We may safely assume that, providing he has locked his car,
the man knows that he has done so, viz., that P. Even so, it is
not absolutely clear whether he is sure that he has or has not.
(We should need to know more about him and his relationship
with his wife to say.)

So what this example suggests is that a man could know
that P and yet not be sure that P.[1]

From *Analysis,* 27 (1966), 1–11. Reprinted by permission of the author
and Basil Blackwell.

[1] It also suggests that checking up on something does not invariably
require or imply doubt on the part of the checker with regard to what
he checks up on, nor does it imply or require this to make his action
rational. Security procedures at banks, routine daily inspections on air-
craft, etc., show that this is so.

The next example is less equivocal.

Example 2

MR. REA (*the new librarian*): What did we do with our copies of
W. J. Locke's novels, Miss Tercy?

MISS TERCY: Oh!—I'm not absolutely sure. I *think* we may have
sold them for pulp.

MR. REA: But you're not sure?

MISS TERCY: Well, no, not really, Mr. Rea. I *think* we did. It was
several years ago—well, I think it was. Shall I just go
and . . . (*She leaves.*)

MR. REA: ?

MR. GEE: Oh, that's what'll have happened. She's got a memory
like an elephant.

MR. REA: Well, why is she so . . . so . . . ?

MR. GEE: Anxious? Uncertain? I don't know. Perhaps it's her age
—she isn't sure about anything. But she knows everything about this library. What did she say—they may
have been pulped? Well, you may be certain that's
what'll have happened to them.

This conversation piece shows that a person may be judged
both to know something to be the case, viz., that P, and yet
not be sure that P. For although Miss Tercy's lack of certainty
is, perhaps, neurotic and treated as such, it is also treated as
real. She really isn't sure. It isn't that she is simply prone to
hedge.

The next example is more ambitious.

Example 3

TOM: Right. You won the noughts-and-crosses. Now we'll have a
quiz: English history.

JEAN: Oh! No! I don't *know* any English history.

TOM: Don't be silly, everyone does. You must have done some at
school?

JEAN: They don't teach English history at French-Canadian schools.

Tom: Really? Well, this will be educational for you. And it's time I won something. Ready?

Jean: O.K. I'll just guess. Then I'll ask you some questions on French-Canadian history!

Tom: Yes. Well: sixpence on the first question, shilling on the second, one and six on the third and so on up to five bob?

Jean: Why not?

Tom: Right. First question, for sixpence: when did William the Conqueror land in England?

Jean (*hesitantly*): Ten sixty-six.

Tom: There you are!

Jean: Well, well! Ten sixty-six and all that?

Tom: Yes! Yes—for a shilling: whom did he defeat and kill when he landed?

Jean: Oh! Oh. (*Pause.*) Oh—I don't know.

Tom: It's easy. Kids' stuff.

Jean: I told you.

Tom: Harold! Whom had Harold himself defeated just before the Battle of Hastings?

Jean: I'm glad this isn't for real money. (*Pause.*) Frederick?

Tom: Frederick? No. Harald Hadraga. That's—ah?—two bob. For another two bob—um?—um? Well—moving on a bit then: when did Henry the Eighth die?

Jean (*pause*): He had six wives?

Tom: Yes.

Jean: Oh, I don't know. (*Pause.*) Fifteen seventy-seven?

Tom: Bad luck! Fifteen *forty*-seven. What about Elizabeth?

Jean: Oh! Ah . . . Elizabeth. Elizabeth. Tsst! Ooh . . . Mmm . . . Sixteen-oh-three?

Tom: Yes! Now tell me you haven't done any history!

Jean: No, really.

Tom (*sarcastically*): That was just a guess, was it?

Jean: Well, I don't know. Perhaps I picked that up on a Shakespeare course or somewhere. We didn't do all these kings and queens. Anyway—you owe me . . . ?

Tom: You owe *me*—four bob take away two and six—one and six. For *three* bob, when did James the First die?

Jean: James the First?

TOM: James Stuart, the Sixth of Scotland and the First of England. The first Stuart. He came after Elizabeth.

JEAN: Oh . . . Ah . . . James the First. So he's sixteen-oh-three to . . . to . . . sixteen-oh-three. Sixteen twenty-five?

TOM: Yes! Look here, you must have done these people!

JEAN: Well, I certainly don't remember. As far as I can tell I'm just guessing. And don't think you're going to get me to double up or anything like that!

TOM: I wouldn't dream of it; I owe you one-and-six. Well—this is giving you a chance: Charles the First?

JEAN: When did he get on and off his English throne?

TOM: Yep. He's the next. This is for three-and-six.

JEAN: Ah . . . the *next?* Charles the First? So that's sixteen . . . What was it, sixteen twenty-five? to . . . (*Pause.*) Sixteen-oh-three, sixteen twenty-five—sixteen forty-nine?

TOM: Well, I—

JEAN: Is that right?

TOM: You wouldn't like to double your stake on that?

JEAN: *Oh* no! Is it right, though?

TOM: Yes. No more clues. Um. (*Thinks.*) Oh! Easy: Victoria. When did she ascend the throne?

JEAN: Ah . . . Victoria? Victoria. Victoria. About eighteen twenty?

TOM: What date?

JEAN: Eighteen twenty.

TOM: Hmm. When did she die?

JEAN: Ah! Ah . . . the Victorian Age. Um . . . Eighteen ninety-eight?

TOM: No. She's eighteen thirty-seven to nineteen-oh-one. You're slipping. All right then. Last question. For five shillings: Edward the Seventh came to the throne in nineteen-oh-one. When did he die?

JEAN (*thinking*): Nineteen-nineteen?

TOM: No. Nineteen-ten. That's the last three wrong. Let's see, that's four bob, four and six, five bob, take away five bob— nine and six.

JEAN: Well, there you are. Now do you believe me?

TOM: Well, no. You don't know much, that's true. But besides ten sixty-six, you got all the questions right about the Tudor and Stuart kings—apart from Henry the Eighth.

JEAN (*reflectively*): Yes.

TOM: And even there you got a kind of near mnemonic miss. You know you must have done them at some time. You couldn't just have been guessing, Jean, could you?

JEAN: No, I don't suppose . . . . Yes, you know—come to think of it—I think I remember I *did* once have to learn some dates. . . .

TOM: Ah, yes!

JEAN: Some kings and queens. Perhaps it *was* these. As a punishment I think it was. But I'd quite forgotten about it, really.

TOM: Oh . . .

JEAN: Yes, I think it *was* these—but *really—*

TOM: No, no, no—I believe you. Freudian forgetting, I expect.

Like the others this is not of course a real-life example, and this time we should consider whether it is a possible one, i.e., whether it is a conversation that could take place, and, if it could and did, whether its participants would be right in concluding, as they do, that the Jean-figure did know some English history.

Clearly such a conversation might take place, and I shall temporarily assume that the participants' conclusion would be correct if it did. I shall also assume for the sake of simplicity that Jean was sincere in everything he said and that the questions about the Tudor and Stuart monarchs that he got right he would have got right without any prompting, cues, or clues at all. For if we allow this as a possibility, then we should have to say about our hypothetical example that prior to the quiz, or at very least during the quiz but before hearing Tom's comments on each correct answer, Jean *did* know some English history, viz., that William landed in 1066, Elizabeth died in 1603, etc. In particular, he knew, e.g., the date of James I's death, viz., 1625; that is to say, he knew that James I died in 1625, that P.

And yet of course, although in this situation Jean knew that P, he was not certain, or sure, or confident that P. Indeed he was fairly certain that his answer to the question was wrong, i.e., that not-P, since he believed it to be a pure guess in a situation where only one of many such guesses could be correct.

Moreover, though he was not sure that P, Jean would not have had any grounds for being sure—or, at least, as he was not aware of them, i.e., of having learned that P, etc.—he would not have been justified in being sure, etc., that his answer was right, viz., that P, had he been sure. For although he had at some stage learned that P, he had quite forgotten that he had done so, and was, indeed, quite sure that he had not. (Of course, when we *are* quite sure about such matters, but cannot remember learning about them, we characteristically infer that, since we are sure, we *must* have learned though we have forgotten doing so. But if Jean were both sure, e.g., that James I had died in 1625, and yet sure that he had never learned or heard of or read the date, he would have no right, no good or adequate reason or justification for being sure that it was 1625 or whatever—unless, for whatever reason, his 'intuitions' about such matters invariably turned out to be right, and he knew this.)

So if Example 3 is a possible one it shows that neither being sure that P nor having the right to be sure that P, can be necessary conditions of knowing that P.[2] Indeed, it shows that a man may know that P even though he is *neither* sure that P, and is indeed fairly sure that not-P, *nor* justified in being sure, etc., that P!

This perhaps is surprising. Certainly it contradicts most of what philosophers have had to say about knowledge. Moreover it raises further problems. So, before concluding by discussing a couple of these problems, I want to consider whether and, if so, why, the conclusion that Jean did know some English history is correct.

[2] That is not to say that one is not characteristically or paradigmatically sure of what one knows. But if being sure is a necessary condition, one cannot know unless one is sure. But cf. Cohen's remark, 'Claims to Knowledge', *Arist. Soc. Supp. Vol.* XXXVI (1962), '. . . if . . . confidence that p is *never* a necessary condition of knowledge that p . . .' (p. 46, my italics).

Since the example is a fabricated one we may properly assume that the participants are right as to the facts, i.e., that they are right in thinking that, e.g., James died in 1625, that Jean had learned this at some time, etc. Given this, then, if the conclusion that Jean knew is one that English speakers who shared this information would generally tend to come to, Jean did indeed know and this conclusion is correct. For, ultimately, whether he 'knows' is a question of what 'know' means, which in turn is very much a matter of when, in what situations, English speakers say or would say that someone knows or does not know. Tom's conclusion, which Jean himself finally accepts, viz., that Jean did know some English history, did know, e.g., the date of James' death, is one, I think, that similarly placed English speakers would make, and is therefore correct.

However, whether we say Jean does or does not know is not simply a matter of appealing to one's intuition and then checking this against the result of some Naessian survey. We can provide reasons for our judgment that he knows—and weigh considerations which seem to tell against it—and this is what Tom and Jean do. After some discussion they agree:

(i) That Jean's answers show that he has—he *must* have—*learned* some English history, viz., that which constitutes or, more probably, includes the answers to those questions he got right, which seems to be, almost exclusively, the dates of the Tudor and Stuart monarchs. I.e., at some stage he must have learned that James I died in 1625, etc. He did not get these answers right by sheer fluke or chance (or—a possibility they did not even bother to rule out—as a result of some mysterious intuition).

(ii) They also show that he has *not forgotten* all the history, all the dates, that he must have learned—even though he *has* forgotten that he has learned them (it). For he produces various correct dates when asked, and does so in such a way and sufficiently often to preclude the possibility that he might simply be guessing and not remembering—even though he is inclined to think that he *is* guessing.

(iii) So he *remembers* some history, and hence he knows some history, including, e.g., that P.

Of course, Jean's knowledge of English history is a poor thing, sparse, uncertain, unwitting, and therefore unimpressive and of little use. But that is not to say that, at the time of the quiz, it is wholly gone, totally forgotten, i.e., that it does not exist.

Although the quiz reveals that Jean does know some English history, he does not know that he knows any until after Tom has told him that certain of his answers are correct.[3] E.g., when asked, Jean knew the date of James I's death, viz., that P, but he did not know that he knew this. For he did not think that he knew the date of James's death and was indeed quite sure that he did not and that he would therefore have to make a guess at it. Moreover, had he been sure that he knew the date, and yet still sure, as he was, that he had never learned it (and sure that if he *had* ever seen or heard or read it, it had left no 'impression', and had not 'registered', etc.), he would certainly have had no right to be sure that he knew the date. But this last point is a complication. Jean was not sure that he knew the date of James's death for he was sure that he did not know it, and, having forgotten that he had learned it, and indeed being quite sure that he had never learned it, he did not have the right to be sure that he knew this date.

But although this conclusion is correct, the account above of why Jean did not know that he knew, e.g., that P, is incomplete and in such a way as to seem paradoxical. For it appears to reintroduce at the second level (knowing that one knows

---

[3] Hence a gap can appear between knowing that P and knowing that one knows that P. That it does sometimes appear is suggested by remarks made when the gap closes, *cf*. 'I didn't know I knew that—you know, that the molecular weight of oxygen was sixteen'. But that it can has been denied e.g. by Richard Taylor, 'Knowing what one knows', *Analysis*, 16.2 (December 1955, p. 65), and queried e.g., by Michael Clark (*Analysis*, December 1963, p. 48).

that P) precisely those conditions for knowing which, I have argued, are not necessary conditions for knowing at the first level (knowing that P) or at any level at all.

In fact, of course, no paradox is involved here. For to say that being sure and having the right to be sure are not necessary conditions of knowing that . . . is not to say that it is possible to know that ϕ without satisfying these conditions for any value of 'ϕ', but only that one can know that ϕ without satisfying these conditions for at least one value of 'ϕ'. (Cf. footnote 1.)

Even so, the account of why Jean does not know that he knows any English history, including, e.g., that P, is incomplete, and we can remove the air of paradox by seeing both why we want to say that Jean knows at the first level—even though he is not sure and does not have the right to be sure (that P) and that these considerations do not exist or operate at the second level in this particular case.

We conclude that Jean knows some English history, e.g., the dates of some of the Tudor and Stuart monarchs, because his answers, though different, are *right* sufficiently often and in such a way as to persuade us that he has learned these dates and not simply guessed them, i.e., they persuade us that he has learned some history and has remembered some. And, since he remembers some, he knows some, even though he is not sure, etc. In contrast, had the questions in the quiz been framed slightly differently, 'Do you *know* when . . . ?' (or 'Are you going to have a guess?'), Jean would have consistently and no doubt wearily replied 'No, I don't know. I'll guess. Was it . . . ?' *even when he did know the date.*

Of course Jean would talk in this way precisely because he is sure that he has never come into contact with any English history and is, therefore, quite sure that he does not know any. But this does not mean that a man could not know that he knew that . . . unless he was sure that he knew and he had the right to be sure. For let us consider a slightly different case in which a man is not sure that he knows any English history and does not have the right to be sure that he knows any as it is years since he did any history. Despite this, he says at the

beginning of a history quiz, quite modestly but firmly, that he
does know a little history. He is then asked ten questions, and
on the four occasions that he does know the date he says,
sometimes after a little hesitation, that he does know it and
gives the correct date, and when he does not know he says
that he does not. I think we should have to say of such a man
that he did know a little history, and that he knew that he
knew a little history. (We could hardly say of him that he
didn't know that he knew any history.)

So it is perhaps not merely Jean's not being sure, or his not
having the right to be sure, or even his not believing that he
has the right to be sure, that he knows the answers to any of
the questions that Tom asks him, that debars him from knowing that he knows any English history, or knowing that he
knows, e.g., that P. It is rather that (being quite sure he does
not know any) he says at the beginning of the quiz that he
does not, and would say that he did not know the answer
to any particular question in the quiz even when he did. It is
because he gets or would get the answers to the 'Do you
know . . . ?' questions wrong (and certain of the dates right)
that we say that he is not *aware*, does not realize, i.e., he does
not know, that he knows any history.[4]

Secondly: although at the time of the quiz Jean knew some
English history, viz., a few dates, before he realised—before he
knew—that he knew some, he had no *right* to say that he knew.
It would, in some way, have been improper for him to say,
e.g., that he knew that James died in 1625, prior to his learning
that this was indeed the case, i.e., that he knew. That is not
to say that different circumstances could not excuse, justify, or
even make praiseworthy Jean's saying this, but only that,
whatever the circumstances, a *prima facie* objection remains,
i.e., to claiming that one knows that P when one is not sure
that P or does not believe that one knows that P.

Cohen (see footnote, p. 176), who distinguishes statements

---

[4] But could a man know that he knew some history if he were not
merely unsure that he did, but pretty sure that he did not? Apparently
not. But why not?

as acts, statements as the contents of a subclass of such acts, and propositions (I am unable to make the latter distinction), argues that a man's lack of confidence that P does not *eo ipso* render his act of 'making the statement' that he knows that P unjustifiable, i.e., *morally* unjustifiable (p. 39), which of course is correct. And for him the only other question of justifiability that can arise is whether the proposition that is 'uttered' when the statement is made is true or not. But although special circumstances could, e.g., make Jean's claiming that he knew that P morally justifiable, that is not to say that the *prima facie* objection would not remain to his doing so or that it would not have to be met and overcome if his action were to be morally justified. It is this *prima facie* impropriety, which Cohen misses or dismisses and which remains even when what Jean says happens to be true, that I want to explain.

Those who claim that being sure and having the right to be sure are necessary conditions of knowledge can give a clear explanation though, as I have argued, an incorrect one. They can say that had Jean claimed that he knew that P, what he said would have been improper in that it would have been false. But, on my thesis, had he said this, it would have been true; Jean did know the date of James's death, and yet it would nonetheless have been improper for him to say this. Why?

The answer is of course simply that, although Jean did know that P, he neither knew that he knew that P nor did he believe that he knew. In exactly the same way, Jean would have had no right *prima facie* to state, assert, claim—or, for that matter, agree, admit, concede, etc.—that P either, since although he did know that P he did not know that he knew that P nor did he believe that he knew that P (for he was neither sure that P, nor did he have the right, or believe that he had the right to be sure that P).

This account presupposes that it is *prima facie* improper for a man to state, etc., that he knows that P, or that P, or whatever, unless he believes that he does know that what he says is true, and his belief that he knows this is confident, sure, certain, etc., and, he believes, well-grounded or reasonable, etc. This may be true, but how so?

(i) If a man states, etc., that P, or that he knows that P, or whatever, i.e., states or concedes, etc., whatever he does state or concede (without qualification, 'as if it were a fact'), his doing this implies in some way that he believes that what he says is true, that he is confident that this is so, and that he believes that he has the right to be confident that this is so. (For if he is not sure, etc., he should qualify what he says.) I.e., it implies that he at least *believes* that he knows that what he says is true. But Jean did not believe that he knew that P, and so his stating, etc., that P would have implied something false, and hence would have been *prima facie* improper in this sense.[5]

(ii) If a man does not believe that he knows that P, this may be because he is not sure that P, or not sure that he has the right to be sure that P, or sure that he does not know that P, or sure that he knows that not-P, etc. So if a man does not believe that he knows that P, then, *ceteris paribus,* it is not likely that he *does* know that P and entirely problematic (for most values of 'P') that P. So if he says that he knows that P, what he says is likely to be false either because it is not the case that P or because he does not know that P. Hence, what he says is likely to be improper in this sense. Moreover, and as we have already seen, if a man states, etc., that he knows that P, or P, or whatever, his doing this implies that he at least believes that he knows that what he says is true. So not only does he say something that may very well be false, his doing this implies that he at least thinks he knows that what he says is true, and this is certainly false. But not only is what is implied by his stating that he knows that P, or P, or whatever, false, it is something which, more than anything else he could imply by what he does, would

[5] Of course, what is implied in this kind of way is not always believed by a hearer, nor is it always morally wrong to mislead or to intend to mislead him. But it is *prima facie* wrong.

tend to suggest to others that what he says is true. (Compare what he does, which is to *state*, etc., that he knows that P, with someone's *guessing* that he, the guesser, knows that P. His doing this, viz., guessing that he knows that P, does not imply that he, the guesser, knows or thinks he knows that what he guesses is true. *Au contraire.* So his guessing would not tend to persuade or suggest to a listener who knew what the guesser was doing, viz., guessing, that the guesser did know that he knew that P. It would suggest instead that the guesser was not at all sure that he knew that P.) Thus a man's stating, etc., that he knows that P when he does not believe that he knows this has implications that are themselves false and which suggest to the naïve hearer that he may accept as true what may very well be false, viz., that the speaker knows that P. Such behaviour is intentionally misleading, and, of course, remains so even if, like Jean, the speaker does know that P.

I think this does explain how Jean's stating, etc., that he knew that P, when he did not believe this, would have been *prima facie* improper even though he did know that P. The explanation, which has the advantage of allowing that Jean could know without believing that he knew, also has the advantage of offering an account, and precisely the same account, of the precisely similar impropriety of a man's stating, etc., that P when he does not believe that he knows this. Now as in this case the man does not state or claim or assert, etc., that he *knows* that P, the rival explanation has no application here and so cannot possibly explain the impropriety.

'But', it may now be asked, 'even if it is true that a man's stating, etc., that P somehow implies that he is confident that he knows, and, he believes, properly confident that he knows that P, how does it do this?'

This is not perhaps a question that I ought to try to answer within the confines of this paper, but since it is interesting and difficult, and a problem that the paper leaves me with, I shall very briefly try to say something about it.

It is tempting to say that there is a convention, a linguistic convention, in English and perhaps in other languages too, that one does not state, etc., that P unless one is confident and, one feels, properly confident that one knows that P. So anyone who breaks this convention says something or, perhaps, does something, that is misleading, and if he breaks it deliberately, then he is being deliberately misleading.

But this sketch of an account, though attractive, is not just inadequate but, I suspect, fundamentally incorrect. For it entails that there could be a language with a convention which allowed one to state, etc., that P, even though one did not believe that one knew that P, i.e., a language in which someone's stating that P did not imply that the speaker at least thought he knew that what he said was true, and hence a language in which, if someone did state that P without believing that he knew that P, his doing so would not be regarded as misleading or *prima facie* improper.

The difficulty here is that if there were such a language, we could not understand its users' 'stating', 'asserting', 'claiming', 'conceding', etc., that P, i.e., their saying that P without qualification and as if it were a fact, as *that*. We should rather understand it, if we could understand it at all, as their analogue of our saying 'I don't know whether P or not', but this of course is not a way of saying that P.

The reason for this is that stating, etc., that P, i.e., saying that something is the case, is essentially something that we do to inform. But we cannot hope or try or intend to inform unless we at least believe that we are ourselves informed, i.e., have knowledge. Thus we cannot construe something that a person does as his stating, asserting, etc., i.e., as his saying that something or other is the case, without thinking that either he at least believes he knows what he is talking about and so knows that P, if that is what he says, or he is misleading us and, therefore, his saying that P is at least *prima facie* improper.

To briefly summarise my negative conclusions: neither

believing that P nor, *a fortiori*, being confident, sure, quite sure, or certain that P is a necessary condition of knowing that P. Nor is it a necessary condition of knowing that P that one should have the right to be, or be justified in being, or have adequate grounds for being sure that P. Nor is it a necessary condition that one should *believe* that one has the right to be, etc., sure that P. It is, perhaps, rather that being sure that P, and believing that one has the right to be sure that P, are necessary conditions of *believing* that one knows, and hence of having the *prima facie* right to say that one knows that P.

PART FOUR

DOES KNOWING ENTAIL KNOWING THAT ONE KNOWS?

R. M. Chisholm

The Logic of Knowing

I

Jaakko Hintikka's *Knowledge and Belief** is worth trying to expound in relatively simple English. It is a work on "epistemic logic," or "the logic of knowing," which contains important contributions to epistemology, the philosophy of language, and the philosophy of mind. The author has a rare combination of qualities: technical competence and originality in mathematical logic, sensitivity to ordinary language, and a knowledge of the history of philosophy. But his book is considerably more difficult than it needs to be; its technicality may discourage all but those readers who are interested in modal logic and model sets. I shall try to state clearly some of the things that are done in this book; I shall note certain results that seem to me to be dubious; and I shall comment on some of the author's philosophical presuppositions.

II

For reasons that are not entirely clear, epistemic logic has been confined to a study of the analogies that hold between

---

From *The Journal of Philosophy*, 60, 25 (December 5, 1963), 773–795. Reprinted by permission of the author and *The Journal of Philosophy*.

* Jaakko Hintikka, *Knowledge and Belief: An Introduction to the Logic of the Two Notions*. Ithaca, N.Y.: Cornell University Press, 1962.

knowledge and necessity. We know at least that there is this much of an analogy: from the fact that a proposition is necessary, it follows that the proposition is true, but from the fact that a proposition is true, it does not follow that the proposition is necessary; similarly, from the fact that a proposition is known to be true, it follows that it is true, but from the fact that a proposition is true, it does not follow that it is known to be true. The problem of epistemic logic seems to be: is there any further analogy?

The relations between the logic of necessity and the logic of knowing—between the "alethic" and epistemic modalities—were occasionally discussed in connection with the traditional doctrine of the modal syllogism. One of the most interesting of these discussions may be found in the *Commentary on the Prior Analytics*, included in the collected works of Duns Scotus, but now attributed to "Pseudo-Scotus."[1] This work, to which Hintikka does not refer, may throw some light upon the present book.

Pseudo-Scotus pointed out, among other things, that: (i) for any valid syllogism, if we prefix one of the premises by 'It is known', we can still draw the original conclusion; but (ii) in such a case we cannot draw the result of prefixing the conclusion by 'It is known'. He also noted (iii) that if we prefix either of the premises by 'It is believed', we cannot draw the conclusion as modified by 'it is believed'. He said further (iv) that if we prefix both premises of a valid syllogism by 'it is known', referring to the same knower in each case, we cannot draw the result of prefixing the conclusion by 'It is known'. For, he argued, we must reject the principle: "If the premises are known, the conclusion is known." The knower might have derived one premise from one source and the other from quite a different source, in which case he might not have put 2 and 2 together. Or he might put 2 and 2 together and still not be

---

[1] Duns Scotus, *Quaestiones: In Librum Primum Priorum Analyticorum*, in Vol. II of *Opera Omnia*, edited by Vivès. On the status of "Pseudo-Scotus," see I. M. Bochenski, "De consequentiis scholasticorum earumque origine," *Angelicum*, 15 (1938): 92–109.

clever enough to realize what they jointly imply. If the conclusion can be known only by inference, then, Pseudo-Scotus says, the conclusion is no better known than is the validity of the inference by means of which it is derived (*op. cit.*, p. 175). Here, then, we would seem to have a significant disanalogy between knowledge and necessity: from the fact that the premises of a valid argument are known to be true, it does not follow that the conclusion is known to be true; but from the fact that the premises of a valid argument are necessary, it does follow that the conclusion is necessary.

In *An Essay in Modal Logic* (Amsterdam, 1951), G. H. von Wright contended that the analogy between knowledge and necessity does not break down at this point. And indeed he proposed a system in which alethic principles, such as those of C. I. Lewis's strict implication system S4, might be transformed into principles of epistemic logic. Von Wright's system suggests that we have epistemic analogues not only of the principle that (*a*) if *p* entails *q* and if it is necessary that *p*, then it is necessary that *q*, but also of such principles as: (*b*) if it is necessary that *p* and necessary that *q*, then it is necessary that *p* and *q*; (*c*) whatever is a logical law is necessary; and (*d*) if it is necessary that *p*, then it is necessary that it is necessary that *p*. In each case the alethic principle may be transformed into a true epistemic principle by replacing 'necessary' with 'verified' or 'known to be true'. But von Wright left undecided how we are to interpret his term 'verified', or 'known to be true'. If these epistemic principles are taken to refer to the actual knowledge of some particular person, say John, at any particular time, then they would seem to be false or at least problematic. One may object, as Pseudo-Scotus did, to (*a*) and go on to note: (*b*) since people notoriously refrain from putting 2 and 2 together, we cannot be sure that if John knows that *p* and John knows that *q*, then John also knows that *p* and *q*; (*c*) we cannot say of John, or of anyone else, that every logical law is something he knows to be true; and (*d*) the thesis, "Whatever John knows is something that John knows that he knows" has been one of great controversy in epistemology.

It is in this context that we may try to understand Hintikka's book. Hintikka defends epistemic versions of Lewis's alethic principles; he says, however, not that they are true, but that they are "self-sustaining," an expression to which we shall return. The principles are defended by means of the technique of "model sets and model systems," a technique which the author has developed in connection with alethic modal logic.

The first three chapters set forth this general technique. The fourth applies the result of the technique to certain philosophical problems (e.g., "Moore's paradox") involving knowledge and belief. The fifth offers a proof that the sentence "knowing implies knowing that one knows" is "self-sustaining," and relates this proof to the traditional problem of knowing that one knows. The sixth and final chapter ("Knowledge, Belief, and Existence") introduces quantification into epistemic logic, and the results are applied, once again, to traditional problems of philosophy.

III

The technique of "model sets and model systems," as it is developed here, is essentially the following.

We may think of a "model set" as a set of sentences describing some logically possible state of affairs. One task for logic would be to lay down conditions that sentences must fulfill if they are to be admitted into any such set. Among such conditions are these: if a given model set contains a certain sentence p, then it must not also contain the negation of p; if it contains a conjunction, it contains each of the conjuncts; if it contains a disjunction, it contains at least one of the disjuncts; if it contains the negation of the negation of p, it contains p; if it contains the negation of a conjunction, it contains the negation of at least one of the conjuncts; if it contains the negation of a disjunction, it contains the negations of each of the disjuncts. The rules or conditions of admission will also specify conditions under which quantified sentences may be admitted into such a set. Thus if the set contains a sentence beginning with the prefix, 'There exists an x', it will contain a sentence that is like the formula following the prefix, except for containing a 'free individual symbol' in each of the places where the formula contains 'x'—the same symbol in each of the places. As we shall see, there are other conditions for quantified sentences, as well as conditions for identities (for example, that no sentence of the form "It is false that a is identical with a" may be admitted).

If a set of sentences can be "imbedded" into a model set, satisfying these (and certain other) conditions, then that set of sentences is consistent. Hence the author says that the concept of a model set is "a very good formal counterpart to the informal idea of a (partial) description of a possible state of affairs."

Let us consider, then, a model set μ of sentences satisfying conditions such as those just described. We may say that an *alternative* to μ is any model set of sentences satisfying at least these same conditions. Any *set* of such alternatives to a given model set is a *model system*. Thus if we think of the sentences in μ as partially describing one possible world, we may think of the sentences in alternatives to μ as partially describing other possible worlds; hence a model system may be thought of as describing a set of possible worlds. And therefore one approach to "alethic" modal logic—to the logic of necessity and possibility—is to lay down conditions of admissibility into model systems. The author has developed this approach to alethic logic in considerable detail in other writings; the technical part of the present book may be thought of as an application to epistemic logic of the techniques thus developed. The book might have been clearer for some readers had the author first presented this approach to alethic logic. I shall try, then, to set forth this approach, at least in general terms, and then note the transition to epistemic logic.

Just as we may set forth conditions that sentences must fulfill in order to be admitted into a given model set, we may set forth conditions of admissibility into a system of model sets—a model system which we may think of as describing a set of possible worlds. These conditions may be thought of as explicating the laws of logical necessity and logical possibility. I shall formulate six such conditions, oversimplifying to a certain extent. I choose these six in particular because their epistemic analogues play a central role in the present book. After each I shall note an instance of the general truth that the condition is designed to capture.

1. $(C \cdot M^*)$ If "It is possible that p" is contained in a model set μ, then p is contained in at least one of the alternatives to μ.

If it is logically possible that it is raining, then there is at least one possible world in which it is raining.

2. $(C \cdot N)$ If "It is necessary that p" is contained in a model set μ, then p is contained in μ.

If it is logically necessary that either it is raining or it is not raining, then either it is raining or it is not raining.

3. $(C \cdot N^*)$ If "It is necessary that p" is contained in a model set μ, then p is contained in each alternative to μ.

If it is logically necessary that either it is raining or it is not raining, then in every possible world either it is raining or it is not raining.

4. $(C \cdot \sim N)$ If "It is not necessary that p" is contained in a model set μ, then "It is possible that not-p" is contained in μ.

If it is not necessary that it is raining, then it is possible that it is not raining.

5. $(C \cdot \sim M)$ If "It is not possible that p" is contained in a model set μ, then "It is necessary that not-p" is contained in μ.

If it is not possible that it is both raining and not raining, then it is necessary that it is not both raining and not raining.

6. $(C \cdot NN^*)$ If "It is necessary that p" is contained in a model set μ, then "It is necessary that p" is contained in each alternative to μ.

What is necessary in this world is necessary in all possible worlds.

Suppose now we take the formula '$K_a p$' to mean that a certain person a knows the sentence p to be true. Suppose we take '$P_a p$' to mean that, for all that a knows, it is possible that p is true. The latter expression, according to the author, may also be read as: "It does not follow from what a knows that not-p." And let us restrict ourselves to what the person a knows on some particular occasion or at one particular time (so that we will not have to take account of the fact that at one time he may know that p is true and at another time not know that p is true). We can thus consider what he knows on that occasion—and we may consider the "epistemic alternatives" to what he then knows, these alternatives being all of those possible states of affairs which are compossible with the totality of what he then knows. We are now in a position to develop an "epistemic logic" in analogy with the modal logic just described.

The six conditions that follow, then, may be derived from the six alethic conditions just listed, if we replace 'it is necessary' ('N') by 'a knows' ('K_a'), and replace 'it is possible' ('M') by 'it is possible for all a knows' ('P_a'). I shall use the author's labels but not his symbolism. Once again I shall illustrate, in somewhat intuitive terms, what these conditions come to if we interpret them in a perfectly straightforward way. But it is essential to note that the author does not interpret them in this straightforward way, and that he makes use of other epistemic principles.

1. $(C \cdot P^*)$ If "It is possible, for all a knows, that p" is contained in a model set μ, then p is contained in at least one of the alternatives to μ.

If it is possible, for all *a* knows, that it is raining, then it is raining in one of those worlds which are compossible with what *a* knows.

2. (C · K)   If "*a* knows that *p*" is contained in a model set *μ*, then *p* is contained in *μ*.

If *a* knows that it is raining, then it is raining.[2]

3. (C · K*)   If "*a* knows that *p*" is contained in a model set *μ*, then *p* is contained in each alternative to *μ*.

If *a* knows that it is raining, then it is raining in all of those worlds which are compossible with what *a* knows.

4. (C · ∼ K)   If "It is false that *a* knows *p*" is contained in a model set *μ*, then "It is possible, for all *a* knows, that not-*p*" is contained in *μ*.

If it is false that *a* knows that it is raining, then it is possible for all *a* knows that it is not raining.

(Sometimes an utterance of "It is false that *a* knows that *p*," or "*a* does not know that *p*," presupposes that the speaker does know that *p*, but at other times not; here we must take "It is false that *a* knows" in the second sense.)

These first four conditions should give no pause. But the two that follow are something else again.

5. (C · ∼ P)   If "It is false that it is possible, for all *a* knows, that *p*" is contained in a model set

---

[2] Thus Pseudo-Scotus had said that any proposition whatever is such that it follows from the result of prefixing it by 'know' ("Quia quaelibet propositio sequitur ad seipsam modificatam isto modo *scire*, sicut sequitur, *Scio B esse A; igitur B est A*"). He contrasted 'know' with 'think' (opinor) and 'it seems' (apparet) in this respect. *Op. cit.*, p. 175.

> μ, then "a knows that it is false that p" is contained in μ.

If the sentence that it is raining is not consistent with what a knows to be true, then a knows that it is not raining.

Taken in any such straightforward sense the principle is itself false as we have noted. The negations of many of the theorems of mathematics, for example, are incompatible with what I know, since they are incompatible with any proposition whatever, but, unfortunately, most of them are not such that I know them to be false. Hintikka says, however, that there is an important sense in which I may be said *virtually* to know all of the truths of logic and mathematics: I *would* know them, in a straightforward sense, if only I were sufficiently clever to be able to carry out the implications of what I do know. His logic of knowing is thus concerned with "virtual knowledge"— a concept to which I shall return.

6. $(C \cdot KK^*)$ If "a knows that p" is contained in a model set μ, then "a knows that p" is contained in each alternative to μ.

If a knows that it is raining, then, in all of those worlds which are compossible with what a knows, a also knows that it is raining.

Here the use of simple English may suggest a possible ambiguity which the author's symbolism obscures. In the previous conditions cited, the expression 'It is possible, for all a knows, that p' seemed to mean simply: (A) p is logically compatible with the set of all of those sentences t such that a knows that t is true. But with this final principle, we seem to have shifted to: (B) p is logically compatible, not only with the set of all those sentences t such that a knows that t is true, but *also* with the sentence that a *does* know the members of this set of sentences to be true. If (A), and not (B), is the proper interpretation of 'It is possible, for all a knows, that p' (i.e., '$P_a p$'), then it is not at all clear that we should impose

this final condition $(C \cdot KK^*)$. There is some reason for believing that the author vacillates between these two possible
interpretations of '$P_a p$'. As we shall see, this problem of interpretation, and the status of $(C \cdot KK^*)$, is crucial when he
turns to the problem of "knowing that one knows."

We are now in a position to see how the author demonstrates
his particular epistemic principles. Each proof is a *reductio ad
absurdum:* to prove that a sentence is true, he proves that the
assumption of the sentence's negation violates one of his conditions of admission. The following, for example, is his proof
that the knowledge of a conjunction is implied by the knowledge of each of its conjuncts—or, more accurately, that such
knowledge is "virtually implied."

(1) $K_a p \cdot K_a q$ is a member of μ.	Assumption
(2) $\sim K_a (p \cdot q)$ is a member of μ.	Assumption
(3) $P_a \sim (p \cdot q)$ is a member of μ.	2, $C \cdot \sim K$
(4) $\sim (p \cdot q)$ is a member of an alternative μ^* to μ.	3, $C \cdot P^*$
(5) $K_a p$ is a member of μ.	1, Condition on conjunction
(6) $K_a q$ is a member of μ.	1, Condition on conjunction
(7) p is a member of μ^*.	5, $C \cdot K^*$
(8) q is a member of μ^*.	6, $C \cdot K^*$
(9) Either $\sim p$ is a member of μ^* or $\sim q$ is a member of μ^*.	4, Condition on negated conjunction

But the conjunction of (7), (8), and (9) violates the first condition mentioned above—namely, that if a model set μ contains a given sentence then it does not also contain the
negation of that sentence. Hence the two assumptions, con-
stituting (1) and (2), are not cotenable, and therefore the first
(virtually) implies the second.

By this technique, Hintikka is able to transform the modal
theorems of C. I. Lewis's system S4 of strict implication into

epistemic sentences. Given Hintikka's interpretation of the sentences that result, his epistemic logic is entirely plausible—with the possible exception of the analogues of such theorems as Lewis's "If a sentence is necessary, then necessarily it is necessary."

IV

Let us now face the difficult problem of interpreting these epistemic sentences.

In the proof just cited, Hintikka professes to prove not that the knowledge of a conjunction is implied by the knowledge of its conjuncts, but only that such knowledge is "virtually implied." What does it mean, then, to say that one sentence "virtually implies" another? Hintikka tells us that one sentence "virtually implies" another provided that the conditional having the former sentence as antecedent and the latter sentence as consequent is a sentence that is "self-sustaining." And he tells us that a sentence is "self-sustaining" provided that its negation is "indefensible." (His proofs thus consist in showing, with respect to the sentences he wishes to prove, that their negations are "indefensible.") What does it mean, then, to say of a sentence that it is "indefensible"? The author leaves this difficult question pretty much to the reader.

I think that the following will illustrate, but not define, what he has in mind. A sentence is indefensible if: (i) it is logically false; or (ii) it says of some person that that person believes some sentence that is indefensible; or (iii) it says of some person, who believes a sentence that is not indefensible, that he does not believe, or that he disbelieves, some of the logical consequences of that sentence; or (iv) it says of some person that he does not know to be true some of the sentences that are logical consequences of sentences he does know to be true; or (v) it says of some person that he does not believe a certain sentence the negation of which is indefensible; or (vi) it implies a sentence saying of some person that that person believes that some *other* person believes some sentence which is

indefensible, or does not believe a certain sentence the negation of which is indefensible. . . . Thus Hintikka tells us that
indefensible sentences are sentences that "depend for their
truth on somebody's failure (past, present, or future) to follow
the implications of what he knows (or believes) far enough."

The word 'indefensible', therefore, is misleading, for the
sentences that Hintikka calls "indefensible" may be true and,
indeed, may be known to be true. If I know that you do not
accept some of the consequences of some of the things that
you know or that you believe something that is logically false,
and if I say as much, then my true sentence is "indefensible."
Ordinarily, however, we would say that what is indefensible,
in such a situation, is not my own sentence, or statement of it
(questions of etiquette aside), but what it is that I am describing—namely, your neglect to draw all of the consequences of
what you know, or your acceptance of something that is logically false. 'Shocking', 'disappointing', or 'epistemically scan-
dalous' might be less misleading.

Perhaps the general character of indefensible sentences can
best be grasped in terms of this figure: they are sentences that
would be false in a world populated only by perfect logicians
—a world of people whom we might call "L-omniscient." (If
there is a problem of epistemic *akrasia*, we would have to add
that a "perfect logician" is a man who *draws*, as well as *sees*,
all the consequences of everything he knows and believes.)
One way to interpret Hintikka's formulas, then, is to think of
the person denoted by his subscript 'a' as being an inhabitant
of such a world of perfect logicians; in this case, we could
replace his 'self-sustaining' by 'true in every world having only
L-omniscient inhabitants', and replace his 'indefensible' by
'false in every world having only L-omniscient inhabitants'.[3]

[3] Lewis and Langford had noted that there is a "relative" interpretation of 'possible' and 'necessary', according to which 'possible' means
"consistent with everything known," and 'necessary' means "implied by
what is given or known"; C. I. Lewis and C. H. Langford, *Symbolic
Logic* (New York 1932), p. 161. Hintikka's 'K' and 'P' might also be
interpreted by reference to such relative possibility and necessity.

V

Hintikka uses this concept of *indefensibility* to throw interesting light upon "Moore's paradox" and a number of related problems. A sentence of the form

(1) *p*, but I do not believe *p*

does not involve an explicit contradiction; but it is logically odd and seems to involve some kind of mistake; where, then, does its oddity lie? The "paradox" is not confined to the concept of *belief*, since, as Hintikka points out, the following sentence gives rise to similar problems:

(2) *p*, but I do not know whether *p*.

If we change the tense of the principal verb in each of these sentences or if we use the third person instead of the first, the results will not be odd; hence some have attributed the oddity of such sentences to the fact that they are belief-sentences, or knowledge-sentences, which are in the first-person present indicative. Hintikka points out, however, that the following sentence, in the *second* person, also gives rise to similar problems:

(3) *p*, but you do not know that *p*.

What is common to the three sentences?

None of the sentences is itself indefensible, as this concept has been characterized above, but each is related to indefensibility in the following ways. If we prefix the first by 'I believe', the second by 'I know', and the third by 'You know', the result, in each case, will be a sentence that *is* indefensible. Hintikka demonstrates essentially the following points: the first sentence is "doxastically indefensible" (a sentence *s* being "doxastically indefensible for a man to utter" if the sentence saying that he believes *s* to be true is indefensible); the second is "epistemically indefensible" (a sentence *s* being "epistemically indefensible for a man to utter" if the sentence saying he knows *s* to be true is indefensible); and the third is a sentence that it is "epistemically indefensible for one person to address to another" (a sentence *s* being "epistemically indefensible for a person A to address to a person B" if the sentence "B knows *s*" is indefensible).

What is common to the three sentences, in addition to this relation to indefensibility, is the fact that in each case the utterance of the sentence in question "violates" a certain "presumption." The oddity of sentence (1), which is a sentence that is "self-defeating," is due to "the general presumption that the speaker believes or at least can conceivably believe what he says"; the oddity of (2) is due to the fact that, when someone utters a sentence, "we are normally led to expect that he can conceivably know what he is saying is true or that he is at least not depriving himself of this possibility." And the oddity of (3) is due to this fact:

> The first and foremost purpose of addressing a statement to somebody is to inform him of something. Addressing a statement to the person referred to by *a* is in fact often called "letting *a* know something." Now uttering a sentence can only serve this purpose if it is possible for the person to whom it is addressed to know the truth of what he is being told (p. 90).

In each case, the presumption is one that must be fulfilled if utterance of the sentence is to serve any normal purpose.

All of this seems true and important. But the author also assumes—and here he is more difficult to follow—that it throws light upon what he calls "the myth of the self-illumination of certain mental activities." He reasons in somewhat this way: conversation between two people presupposes that the one person hears and understands what the other is saying; the notion of thinking is an analogical extension of the notion of saying ("A soul conversing with herself"); hence

> . . . the fact that one cannot fail to know what one is thinking is an analogical extension of the fact that one cannot fail to know what one is saying. We have also seen that this line of thought shows only that one always knows what one is thinking

in the sense that not knowing it would be epistemically indefensible (p. 95).

The author assumes, in short, that there are certain linguistic
facts—facts about the general "presumptions" of certain types
of utterance—which will help to explain "the myth of self-
illumination." But one could argue equally well—and more
plausibly, it seems to me—that the fact of self-illumination
helps to explain the existence of these presumptions: because
people *do* know, immediately or directly, what it is that they
think and believe, and because, for the most part, they do
have some control over what it is that they say or utter, they
have no excuse for saying things that they don't believe; hence
the "presumption" that people believe what they say.

It is true that these "presumptions" are such that, whenever
a man denies any of the so-called facts of "self-illumination,"
he will be making a very odd statement indeed. And we may
say that the oddity is due, in part, to the presumptions. But
we could *also* say that the presumptions are due to the fact of
"self-illumination." If people don't know what it is that they
believe, why do we presume that they will normally restrict
their statements to statements expressing what it is that they
do believe?

It has been contended by Brentano, Meinong, Prichard, and
many others that if a man *believes* a certain proposition p to
be true, then, by reflecting on his own state of mind, he is
able to come to *know that he believes* that that proposition p
is true. I think that this contention is correct, despite the fact
that a good many philosophers in the present British tradition
reject it. Hintikka considers it in the form of a possible epistemic condition ("If 'a believes q' is a member of μ, then 'a
knows that a believes q' is a member of μ"), and he rejects it,
too. His argument against imposing this condition consists in
assuming something like the following conditional, denying its
consequent, and then denying its antecedent: If, with respect
to every sentence p that a man believes, the man can find out
by reflecting on his own state of mind (Hintikka says by "introspection") *that* he believes that sentence p, then he *also*

ought to be able to find out in a similar manner what it is that
he does *not* know. But I can't imagine how this conditional itself is to be justified.

VI

Chapter Five, entitled "Knowing That One Knows," is one
of the best discussions of the topic that I have read. The historical account of the problem is excellent (except, perhaps,
for the neglect of some of the skeptics); there are many il-
luminating observations concerning the ordinary uses of such
locutions as 'He knows that he knows'; and there is a proof
that knowing "virtually implies" knowing that one knows.

The proof—that $K_a p$ virtually implies $K_a K_a p$—is remarkably
simple:

(1) $K_a p$ is a member of a model set μ.   Assumption
(2) $\sim K_a K_a p$ is a member of μ.   Assumption
(3) $P_a \sim K_a p$ is a member of μ.   (2), $(\text{C} \cdot \sim \text{K})$
(4) $\sim K_a p$ is a member of a model set
     μ^*, which is an alternative to μ.   (3), $(\text{C} \cdot \text{P}^*)$
(5) $K_a p$ is a member of μ^*.   (1), $(\text{C} \cdot \text{KK}^*)$

The conjunction of (4) and (5) violates the condition that no
model set may contain a statement together with its negation;
hence assumptions (1) and (2) are not cotenable; and therefore "knowing" virtually implies "knowing that one knows."

We should remind ourselves, of course, that the sentence
that is thus demonstrated may not be the one with which
philosophers have been concerned when they have asked,
"Can we know without knowing that we know?" The author
professes to prove only that the sentence "He knows but does
not know that he knows" is "indefensible." But, even so, one
remains unconvinced. There is a clear sense in which the other
theorems about what is "indefensible" pertain to a kind of logical negligence; a true indefensible sentence implies that someone has neglected to carry out the logical implications of

something that he knows or believes. But a man who knows
without knowing that he knows would not seem to be guilty of
this type of neglect, unless we could say that knowing *logically*
implies knowing that one knows; and Hintikka does not say
this.

Let us look once again at his conditions of admission, and
let us consider the possible ambiguity, referred to above, in
the expression 'It is possible, for all a knows, that p' ('$P_a p$').
Sometimes, as I have suggested, the author seems to take this
expression ('$P_a p$') to mean (A) that p is logically compatible
with the set of all those sentences which a knows to be true.
But at other times he suggests that it means (B) that p is
logically compatible with the sentence which says, of all of
the sentences which a knows to be true, that they *are* sentences which a knows to be true.[4] The first interpretation
would allow us to say:

(A) $P_a p$ if and only if there is no t such that $K_a t$ and such
that p is not compatible with t.

But the second would allow us to say, more strongly:

(B) $P_a p$ if and only if there is no t such that $K_a t$ and such
that p is not compatible with $K_a t$.

[4] Hintikka seems to have interpretation A in mind when he says that
he will take '$P_a p$' to "mean the same as 'It does not follow from what a
knows that not-p'" (p. 5). But he seems to have interpretation B in
mind when he writes: "If it is consistent of me to say that it is possible
for all that I know, that q is the case, then it must be possible for q to
turn out to be the case without invalidating any of my claims to knowledge; that is, there must not be anything inconsistent about a state of
affairs in which q is true and *in which I know what I say I know*" (p. 17;
cf. pp. 55, 58). The words I have italicized are what suggest interpretation B of '$P_a p$'; if interpretation A were intended, they should be replaced by something like: *"in which the sentences that I say I know are
true."* The general "criterion of consistency" which the author calls
"(A·PKK°)" and by reference to which he defends his rule (C·KK°)
seems clearly to require interpretation B (cf. pp. 17–22).

The distinction between (A) and (B) is obviously tenable, for there may be sentences that are compatible with a given sentence t and yet not compatible with the sentence saying that a knows that t. An obvious—and relevant—example is "It is false that a knows that t." In short, $\sim K_a t$ is incompatible with $K_a t$ but may yet be compatible with t.[5]

And now, having noted that a sentence that is compatible with t may yet be incompatible with $K_a t$, we are led to ask: Could one of the sentences compatible with t but not with $K_a t$ be a sentence that a does *not* know to be false? The consequences of an affirmative answer to this question would be disastrous.

If the following set of assumptions is consistent, or even "defensible," then not only is Hintikka's proof that "knowing virtually implies knowing that one knows" inconclusive, but some of his epistemic principles are themselves mistaken. The assumptions may be put by saying that there is a sentence p having the following properties: a does not know p to be false; p is compatible with every sentence that a knows to be true; and there is a sentence saying, of one of the things that a knows to be true, that he does know it to be true, and p is incompatible with that sentence. Or, in Hintikka's notation:

(1) $\sim K_a \sim p$ is a member of μ.
(2) For every t such that $K_a t$ is a member of μ, p is compatible with t.
(3) $K_a t$ is a member of μ.
(4) p is not compatible with $K_a t$.

If, for the moment, we ignore the distinction between the two possible interpretations of '$P_a p$', we can use Hintikka's principles to derive a contradiction from these assumptions. For:

---

[5] If we replace 'a' by 'the next President', then we may be able to say that "the next President knows that t" does not even virtually imply "the next President knows that the next President knows that t." Hintikka avoids this type of consequence by stipulating, in his final chapter, that a must *know* that he is a.

(5) $P_a p$ is a member of μ.   (1), $(C \cdot \sim K)$, Double
                                           Negation

(6) p is a member of an epis-
     temic alternative μ^* to μ.   (5), $(C \cdot P^*)$

(7) $K_a t$ is a member of μ^*.   (3), $(C \cdot KK^*)$

(8) μ^* is inconsistent.   (4), (6), (7)

We obtain a contradiction if we take the second, third, and fourth assumptions along with interpretation A of '$P_a p$', viz.,

(5′) $P_a p$ is a member of a model set μ if and only if: there is no t such that t is a member of μ and such that p is not compatible with t.

For we may derive:

(6′) $P_a p$ is a member of μ.   (2), (5′)

(7′) p is a member of μ^*.   (6′), $(C \cdot P^*)$

(8′) $K_a t$ is a member of μ^*.   (3), $(C \cdot KK^*)$

(9′) μ^* is inconsistent.   (3), (4), (7′), (8′)

And we obtain a contradiction if we take the first, the third, and the fourth assumptions along with interpretation B of '$P_a p$', viz.,

(5″) $P_a p$ is a member of a model set μ if and only if: there is no t such that t is a member of μ and such that p is not compatible with $K_a t$.

For we derive:

                                           (1), $(C \cdot \sim K)$, Double

(6″) $P_a p$ is a member of μ.   Negation

(7″) $P_a p$ is not a member of μ.   (3), (4), (5″)

The crucial question, then, is whether our four assumptions are consistent. The L-omniscience of a may tempt us to say that (1) is not compatible with (3) and (4). But we cannot prove this incompatibility by appeal to the principle that tells us, with respect to every statement t that a happens to know, that he knows all of the consequences of t. We need a further principle telling us, with respect to every statement t that a happens to know, that a knows all of the logical consequences of the statement *that* he knows t. And this is the very principle which is at issue when we ask whether "knowing virtually implies knowing that one knows."

The "general presumptions" of utterance may seem to support the thesis that "knowing" virtually implies "knowing that one knows." As we have noted, Hintikka attributes the oddity of such sentences as "p but I do not know whether p" to the "general presumption" that, in uttering any sentence p, the man who utters it knows it to be true. If this presumption is itself true, we may also presume that if a man utters "I know that p" then he *knows that he knows* that p. We may say with the author: "all those circumstances which would justify one in saying 'I know' will also justify one in saying 'I know that I know'." But the proper conclusion to be drawn from this, it seems to me, is not that knowing, in any sense, implies knowing that one knows; it is, rather, that if a man does not know that he knows that p (or, perhaps, does not *think* that he knows that p), then he should not *say* that he knows that p, or even say, without hedging, that p. Thus Sextus Empiricus, who professed not to know whether he knew, said that the proper course for any such skeptic is *aphasia*, or "nonassertion," a course which accords with the "general presumption," referred to above.[6] (But this presumption was violated by

[6] It may be recalled that, in setting forth various possible systems of strict implication, C. I. Lewis cited—as an alternative to the principle (C10) enabling one to say that whatever is necessary is necessarily necessary—another principle (C13), which he put in English as "For every proposition p, the statement 'p is self-consistent' is a self-consistent statement"—a principle implying that no statements are necessarily necessary (C. I. Lewis and C. H. Langford, *Symbolic Logic*, pp. 497–499; the reference is to Appendix II, which was written by Lewis). The epistemic analogue of this alternative principle—"For every sentence p, it is possi-

Metrodorus who said, according to Sextus, "We know nothing, nor do we even know the very fact that we know nothing.")

Let us now turn to quantification and epistemic logic.

VII

When Pseudo-Scotus discussed the logic of knowing, he distinguished the use of epistemic operators *in sensu composito* from their use *in sensu diviso*. The sentence "I know that all mules are sterile," he said, is a sentence *in sensu composito,* whereas "All mules are such that I know them to be sterile" is *in sensu diviso.* The epistemic operator 'I know', he pointed out, differs from 'it is true' in the following respect: "It is true that all mules are sterile," *in sensu composito,* is equivalent to "All mules are such that it is true that they are sterile," *in sensu diviso;* but "I know that all mules are sterile," *in sensu composito,* is not equivalent to "All mules are such that I know that they are sterile," *in sensu diviso.* For it is possible, he noted, that I may not believe of *this* mule that it is sterile—a possibility which might arise if I did not know of this particular mule that it is in fact a mule.[7] And Aristotle had pointed out, but in terms of a different example, that "All mules are such that I know that they are sterile," *in sensu diviso,* does not imply "I know that all mules are sterile," *in sensu composito;* for though I may know, of every mule, that it is sterile, I may not know that these are all the mules that there are.[8]

The distinction between the uses of epistemic and other modal operators *in sensu composito* and *in sensu diviso* may be expressed in terms of the occurrence of such operators in quantified sentences. A quantified sentence *in sensu composito* would be one in which the modal operator may be found at

---

ble, for all *a* knows, that it is possible, for all *a* knows, that *p*"—would accord with some versions of Pyrrhonism.

[7] Duns Scotus, *op. cit.,* p. 173. Pseudo-Scotus makes a number of interesting observations, contrasting the logic of "I know," "I believe," "it is true," "it is false," and "it appears," when taken *in sensu composito* and *in sensu diviso.*

[8] *Posterior Analytics,* 74ª, pp. 25–33.

the beginning of the sentence; e.g., "*a* knows that, for every *x*, *x* is material," or "*a* knows that, there exists an *x* such that *x* is material." But there are two quite different possibilities for interpreting a modality *in sensu diviso*. In each case the modal operator would follow the quantifier and thus "divide up" the quantified sentence. But in the one case, it would fall *between* the initial quantifier and its propositional function; as in "For every *x*, *a* knows that *x* is material" and "There exists an *x* such that *a* knows that *x* is material." But in the other case, the modal operator appears *within* the propositional function and, as Pseudo-Scotus puts it, may be thought of as modifying the "copula"; as in "For every *x*, *x* is known by *a* to be material" and "There exists an *x* such that *x* is known by *a* to be material." The difference between these two uses of a modality *in sensu diviso* may seem to be slight, but I think that it is enormous.

When the modality precedes the entire sentence, as it does when taken *in sensu composito,* or when it immediately precedes a propositional function, as it does in the first of the two interpretations of the *sensus diviso*, we may say, following another medieval tradition, that the modality is taken *de dicto*—for it applies either to a "closed sentence" or to an "open sentence." But when it is used *within* an open sentence, as in the second interpretation of the *sensus diviso*, we may say that the modality is taken *de re*.[9]

Hintikka does not discuss the modalities *de re*, but in his final chapter ("Knowledge, Belief, and Existence") he discusses in detail the relations between the epistemic modalities *in sensu composito* and the epistemic modalities in the first interpretation—*de dicto*—of the *sensus composito*. (He does not use any of these medieval terms.) We may understand some of the problems concerned by contrasting the following four types of sentence:

(1) *a* knows that, for every *x*, *x* is material.
(2) For every *x*, *a* knows that *x* is material.

9 Compare von Wright, *op. cit.*, p. 1, and *passim*.

(3) *a* knows that there exists an *x* such that *x* is material.

(4) There exists an *x* such that *a* knows that *x* is material.

The first and third sentences are *in sensu composito*, the second and fourth *in sensu diviso*. The second and fourth involve the difficulties, which Quine has stressed, of quantifying into modal contexts. But Hintikka emphasizes, quite correctly, that a satisfactory epistemic logic must be adequate to the distinction between what we want to say in (1) or (3) and what we want to say in (2) or (4).

When are we justified in asserting an epistemic sentence *in sensu diviso* (2 or 4) as distinguished from one *in sensu composito* (1 or 3)? A few years ago, we could say, *in sensu composito*, "I know that there exists an *x* such that *x* is President Eisenhower's successor," but not, *in sensu diviso*, "There exists an *x* such that I know that *x* is President Eisenhower's successor." Now, however, we can assert both. What has been added?

Hintikka's answer is that we are justified in asserting a sentence, such as (2) or (4), *in sensu diviso*, only when we can say of the *x*, or the *x*'s in question, that *a* knows *what* or *who* it is, or *what* or *who* they are. Now we know *who* President Eisenhower's successor was; but earlier, when we knew only *that* he had a successor, we did not know who he was. Thus we are led to the problem of *knowing who*, and *knowing what*. The problem is partly logical, partly epistemological, and perhaps also partly metaphysical.

First, how are we to put into the notation of quantification a sentence of the form "*a* knows who *b* is"? Hintikka's answer is: we may express such a sentence by saying (*in sensu diviso*) "There exists an *x* such that *a* knows that *x* is identical with *b*."

Secondly, given a sentence, *in sensu composito*, of the form, "*a* knows that there exists an *x* such that *x* is F," what more is needed in order to be able to assert the corresponding sentence *in sensu diviso*—viz., "There exists an *x* such that *a* knows that *x* is F"? Hintikka's answer is: We can pass from such a sentence *in sensu composito* to the corresponding sentence *in sensu diviso* only if we have, as one of our premises, the sentence that *a* knows *which* x is (the) one that is F; i.e., only if we can assert "There exists an x such that *a* knows that x is identical with x and that x is F."[10] In short, we cannot move from an epistemic sentence *in sensu composito* to an epistemic sentence *in sensu diviso* until we are justified in asserting certain epistemic sentences *in sensu diviso*. (Hence it might be held that one aspect of the epistemological problem remains unsolved. For according to *some* epistemologists at any rate, the only statements that are directly evident are certain first-person psychological statements *in sensu composito;* e.g., statements beginning "I believe that," "It seems to me that," "I seem to remember that," etc. And one of the tasks of epistemology is that of formulating principles enabling us to pass from such statements to more objective statements *in sensu diviso*. Russell's early writings on "knowledge by acquaintance and knowledge by description" should be understood in this context. It is no criticism of Hintikka to say that he does not solve this problem, if it is a genuine problem, for his book is on epistemic logic and not on epistemology.)

There is still another aspect of the problem of "knowing who" (and "knowing what"); this aspect of the problem has led some philosophers, and possibly also Hintikka, into metaphysics.

In reply to the question "Who robbed the bank?" one may be able to say, truly, "The man who drove the Buick is the man who robbed the bank" or "Utterson is the man who robbed the bank." Under some conditions these true sentences might constitute an answer to the question "Who robbed the bank?" But under other conditions these same true sentences might not constitute an answer, even if the questioner had not previously known that they were true; in such cases, the questioner might well go on to ask, "Yes, but *who* is the man who drove the Buick?" or "But who *is* Utterson?" More generally, of various true and informative sentences, "*a* is the one who is F," "*a* is the one who is G," "*a* is the one who is H," some but

[10] There is some reason to believe that Hintikka would use two variables in such a sentence and say: "$(Ex)(Ey)K_a((x=y) \cdot Fx)$."

not others will constitute an adequate answer to the question "Who is *a*?" The philosophical problem is: What is it in virtue of which some of these true sentences constitute an adequate answer and some do not? I am inclined to think that this philosophical problem has a pragmatic solution, but others have suggested that its solution can only be metaphysical.

The pragmatic solution would be something like this: The question "Who is *a*?" presupposes a certain context of inquiry, and this context determines which of the various true (and informative) sentences of the form "*a* is the one who . . ." actually constitutes an answer. For example, if I ask you "Who is that man?" my question might be one that could be made more explicit by asking: "Of the people who are coming to the party—the banker, the professor, the artist—which one is that man?" If you make a true statement about the man (e.g., "He is the brother of the man beside him"), but one which does not enable me to infer that he is the banker, or that he is the professor, or that he is the artist, then although you may have made a true and informative statement of the form "That man is the person who is F," you will not have told me *who* he is. We could also say, similarly, that the question "What is *a*?" as well as such statements as "I know *who* he is" and "I wonder *what* that is," presupposes a certain context of discussion or inquiry, and that 'who' and 'what' refer to a position within that context.

The metaphysical solution to our problem is suggested by the traditional treatment of the following sophism: "Do you know Coriscus?" "Yes." "Do you know the man who is approaching?" "No." "But he is Coriscus. Therefore you know who he is and you do not know who he is."[11] The traditional solution is to distinguish between knowing Coriscus *per se* and knowing Coriscus *per accidens:* to know *who* Coriscus is is to know, with respect to certain properties that are *essential* to Coriscus and to no one else, that Coriscus is the man who has these properties; but the property of being the man who is approaching is not essential to Coriscus; hence from the fact

---

[11] See Aristotle's *De Sophisticis Elenchis,* 179^b3.

that you do not know who the man approaching is, it does not follow that you do not know who Coriscus is—despite the fact that Coriscus *is* the man approaching.[12] This view suggests that, no matter how much you may know about Coriscus, if you do not know, with respect to the properties that are essential to Coriscus, that Coriscus is the man who has these properties, then you do not know *who* Coriscus is.

One of Hintikka's footnotes suggests that he might be content with the pragmatic solution of our problem.[13] But his treatment of the problem of "substitutivity of identity" suggests that he may be committed to a metaphysical solution.

VIII

When Pseudo-Scotus takes up the problem of Coriscus, he tells us in effect that the principle of the substitutivity of identity fails in epistemic contexts. The two terms 'Coriscus' and 'the person approaching' denote the same thing; yet if we switch them in the true statement "The person approaching is a person I know to be Coriscus," we derive the false statement "Coriscus is a person I know to be the person approaching."[14] Hintikka's final chapter contains an original and extraordinarily

---

[12] Compare Petrus Hispanus, *Summulae Logicales,* ed., I. M. Bochenski (Turin, 1947), 7.41; Franz Brentano, *Kategorienlehre* (Leipzig, 1933), p. 165. Brentano cites this version of the problem: "Do you know who the person with the mask is?" "No." "Then you don't know who your father is, for the person with the mask is your father."

[13] "In practice it is frequently difficult to tell whether a given sentence of the form '*a* knows who *b* is' or '$(Ex)K_a(b = x)$' is true or not. The criteria as to when one may be said to know who this or that man is are highly variable. Sometimes knowing the name of the person in question suffices; sometimes it does not. Often 'acquaintance' of some kind is required. Our discussion is independent of this difficulty, however . . ." (149*n*).

[14] Strictly, Pseudo-Scotus tells us only that "Venientem cognosco esse Coriscum" does not imply "Coriscum cognosco esse venientem"; *op. cit.,* p. 145. The fact that he uses the first person indicates that here, as elsewhere, he is not sensitive to the charge of "epistemic indefensibility."

interesting discussion of this problem; it is his solution that suggests the metaphysical doctrine of "essentialism" referred to above.

From "Coriscus is (identical with) the person approaching" and "There exists an x such that a knows that x is Coriscus," we are not entitled to infer "There exists an x such that a knows that x is the person approaching." We need the additional premise: "a knows that Coriscus is (identical with) the person approaching." For, as we have already seen, if we have two names or definite descriptions, both referring to one and the same thing, and if one of them occurs in a propositional clause serving as the grammatical object of 'a knows', we may not replace the one by the other unless we can say, of a, that he *knows* that the two terms refer to one and the same thing— or, more accurately, unless we can affirm the result of prefixing 'a knows' to the result of placing 'is identical with' between the two terms.

Here there would seem to be an analogy, once again, between *knowledge* and *necessity:* we may infer "Necessarily a is F" from the conjunction of "Necessarily b is F" and "Necessarily a is identical with b"; but we may not infer "Necessarily a is F" from the conjunction of "Necessarily b is F" and the unmodalized "a is identical with b."

Both types of case present us with a philosophical problem, however, if, as seems evident to some, we are justified in asserting the following version of Leibniz's law:

For every x and every y, if x is identical with y, then whatever is true of x is also true of y.

If a is identical with b, and if it is true of a that necessarily it is F, then should it not also be true of b that necessarily it is F? If Coriscus is the person approaching, and if it is true of Coriscus that a knows him to be Coriscus, then should it not also be true of the person approaching that a knows him to be Coriscus?

One solution to the epistemic version of the problem is to say that "There is an x such that a knows that x is Coriscus" is *not* in fact a truth about Coriscus, and, hence, that the failure of substitutivity in such a sentence is not contrary to Leibniz's law, as formulated above. But Hintikka seems to reject this solution, and properly so, it seems to me. Unless we are willing to accept some version of the doctrine that "the mind cannot get outside the circle of its own ideas," we will want to say that one of the things that are true of Coriscus is that *a* happens to know that he is Coriscus.

Hintikka's solution, as I interpret it, is to reject the version of Leibniz's law that I have formulated. Despite the identity of Coriscus and the person approaching, there are certain things true of Coriscus that are *not* true of the person approaching. How can this be? Oversimplifying, we may say that Hintikka's answer comes to this: Though everything that is true of Coriscus, in *this* world, is also true of the person approaching, in *this* world, there are *other* possible worlds in which some of the things that are true of Coriscus are not true of the person approaching; thus in some of those worlds which are compossible with what *a* knows about this world, the person approaching turns out not to be Coriscus (it is possible, for all *a* knows, that the person approaching is not Coriscus); hence there *are* truths about the person approaching that are not truths about Coriscus.

Such terms as 'Coriscus' are "multiply referential": they refer not only to the Coriscus in this world, but also to the Coriscus's in all of the other possible worlds.[15] "Although 'Dr. Jekyll' and 'Mr. Hyde' in fact refer to one and the same man, they refer to different men in some of the possible worlds we

[15] Hintikka first set forth this view in "Modality as Referential Multiplicity," *Ajatus*, 20 (1957): 49–64. He summarized the view by saying: "When we are doing modal logic, we are doing more than one thing at one and the same time. We are using certain symbols—constants and variables—to refer to the actually existing objects of our domain of discourse. But we are also using them to refer to the elements of certain other states of affairs which need not be realized. . . . If I had to characterize the situation briefly, I should say that the occurrences of our terms in modal contexts are not usually *purely referential*, but rather that they are *multiply referential*" (63–64).

have to discuss in order to discuss what Watson [Utterson?] knows and does not know. For this reason, 'Dr. Jekyll' and 'Mr. Hyde' are not interchangeable here."

This solution involves the following difficulty, it seems to me. If some of the things that are true of Dr. Jekyll in *this* world (supposing for the moment that the story is true) are *not* true of Mr. Hyde in certain *other* possible worlds, and if we take this to mean, *simpliciter,* that there are things true of Dr. Jekyll that are not true of Mr. Hyde, then we presuppose that (in some very difficult sense) Dr. Jekyll in this world is identical with Dr. Jekyll in other possible worlds, and that Mr. Hyde in this world is identical with Mr. Hyde in other possible worlds. But what does it mean to say of something in one possible world that it is identical with something in another possible world?[16] Or, if we do know what it means, how are we to *decide* whether an individual in one possible world is identical with an individual in another? Consider that possible world which differs from this one only in the fact that in that one General De Gaulle has the same weight that I have in this one and in that one I have the same weight that General De Gaulle has in this one; then consider a world in which we similarly exchange other properties; then worlds in which we change more and more properties; then the world in which I have all the properties that General De Gaulle has in this one except that of weight, and in which he has all the properties that I have in this world except that of weight; and finally that

[16] Compare Arnauld's objection to Leibniz: "Moreover, Monsieur, I do not see how, in taking Adam as an example of a unitary nature, several possible Adams can be thought of. It is as though I should conceive of several possible me's; a thing which is certainly inconceivable. For I am not able to think of myself without considering myself as a unitary nature, a nature so completely distinguished from every other existent or possible being that I am as little able to conceive of several me's as to think of a circle all of whose diameters are not equal. The reason is that these various me's are different, one from the other, else there would not be several of them. There would have to be, therefore, one of these me's which would not be me, an evident contradiction." Leibniz, *Discourse on Metaphysics; Correspondence with Arnauld; Monadology* (La Salle, Ill.: Open Court, 1937), p. 94.

possible world (if there is one) in which I have all the properties that General De Gaulle has in this world and in which he has all the properties that I have in this one. Am I identical with General De Gaulle in some of these possible worlds and not in others? If so, in which ones? And how are we to decide?

The doctrine of "essentialism" referred to above might enable us to answer such questions. If there is one set of properties essential to De Gaulle and another set essential to me, then, of course, De Gaulle is identical only with those men in other possible worlds having the first set of properties and I am identical only with those having the second. But we may have to provide for the possibility that in some worlds one and the same person has the properties that are essential to De Gaulle and also the properties that are essential to me, and that in other worlds a number of different people have the properties that are essential to De Gaulle and a number of different people have the properties that are essential to me. For presumably no finite set of properties is itself individuating. If we try to individuate De Gaulle in some other possible world by referring, say, to his spatial relations to the Eiffel Tower, we will only have transferred our problem to that of deciding which, of the various objects in that possible world, is the one that *is* in fact identical with the Eiffel Tower that is to be found in *this* world.

When this doctrine of "referential multiplicity" is applied to epistemic statements, the possible worlds we must consider are restricted to those which are compossible with as much of this world as is known by a. If a knows enough about me to know that p, q, r, and s are true of me in this world, and enough about General De Gaulle to know that p', q', r', and s' are true of him, then, of course, in any world compossible with a's knowledge of this one, p, q, r, and s will be true of me, and p', q', r', and s' will be true of De Gaulle. Hence the first set of sentences will describe conditions that are necessary for being identical with me in other relevant possible worlds, and the second set will describe conditions necessary for being De Gaulle. But will the two sets of sentences describe sufficient conditions? Will they describe conditions sufficient to *individuate* either of us in other possible worlds?

If the first set of sentences describes conditions sufficient for being identical with me in any other epistemically possible world and if the second describes conditions sufficient for being identical with De Gaulle, then it may well turn out that in certain possible worlds I *am* De Gaulle and that in others there are several different De Gaulle's (not merely several people *named* "De Gaulle") and several different *me*'s. What could this possibly mean? Or if the two sets of sentences do not describe sufficient conditions, what more is needed to make a man in another possible world the same person that I am in this one?

The alternatives, it seems to me, are either to say that each thing has its own *haecceity*, which guarantees its uniqueness in every possible world, or to say that *nothing* in any possible world is identical with anything in any other possible world. The latter alternative is incompatible with the doctrine of "referential multiplicity," and the former goes considerably beyond it, entangling us not only in questions of metaphysics, but also in questions of epistemology: How is it possible for *a* to know that he knows the *haecceity* of De Gaulle or Coriscus?

But it is much easier to carp at any attempt to solve a difficult philosophical problem than it is to solve it oneself. One of the best things about this important book is that it is original and constructive, presenting not only new solutions to old problems, but also new problems which should instruct and exercise philosophers for some time to come.[17]

[17] I am indebted to Dagfinn Follesdal for pointing out certain inaccuracies in an earlier version of this article.

Selected Bibliography

Books

1. Armstrong, D. M. *Perception and the Physical World*. London: Routledge & Kegan Paul, 1961.
2. Ayer, A. J. *The Problem of Knowledge*. London: Macmillan, 1956. [Pp. 11–15 of the present volume. Ed.]
3. Chisholm, Roderick M. *Perceiving: A Philosophical Study*. Ithaca, N.Y.: Cornell University Press, 1957.
4. ———. *Theory of Knowledge*. Foundations of Philosophy Series. Englewood Cliffs, N.J.: Prentice-Hall, 1966.
5. Hintikka, Jaakko. *Knowledge and Belief*. Ithaca, N.Y.: Cornell University Press, 1962.
6. Malcolm, N. *Knowledge and Certainty: Essays and Lectures*. Englewood Cliffs, N.J.: Prentice-Hall, 1963. [Pp. 17–32 of the present volume. Ed.]
7. Woozley, A. D. *Theory of Knowledge*. London: Hutchinson, 1949.

Articles

8. Adams, E. M. "On Knowing That," *The Philosophical Quarterly*, 8 (1958), 300–306.
9. Ammerman, R. "A Note on 'Knowing That,'" *Analysis*, 17 (1956–1957), 30–32.
10. Armstrong, J. H. S. "Knowledge and Belief," *Analysis*, 13 (1952–1953), 111–117.

11. Arner, D. "On Knowing," *The Philosophical Review,* 68 (1959), 84–92.

12. Aune, Bruce. "Knowing and Merely Thinking," *Philosophical Studies* (1961), pp. 53–58.

13. Austin, J. L. "Other Minds," *Proceedings of the Aristotelian Society,* Supp. Vol. 20 (1946), 148–187.

14. Barnes, W. H. F. "Knowing," *The Philosophical Review,* 72 (1963), 3–16.

15. Brown, R. "Self-Justifying Statements," *The Journal of Philosophy,* 62 (1965), 145–150.

16. Chisholm, Roderick M. "The Logic of Knowing," *The Journal of Philosophy,* 60 (1963), 773–795.

17. ————. "Sentences About Believing," *Proceedings of the Aristotelian Society,* 56 (1955–1956), 125–148.

18. Clark, Michael. "Knowledge and Grounds: A Comment on Mr. Gettier's Paper," *Analysis,* 24 (1963–1964), 46–48.

19. Danto, Arthur C. "On Knowing That We Know," in Avrum Stroll (ed.), *Epistemology.* New York: Harper & Row, 1967, pp. 32–53.

20. Davis, S. " 'I Know' As an Explicit Performative," *Theoria,* 30 (1965), 157–165.

21. Firth, R. "Chisholm on the Ethics of Belief," *The Philosophical Review,* 68 (1959), 493–506.

22. Geach, P. T. "Assertion," *The Philosophical Review,* 74 (1965), 449–465.

23. Gettier, E. L. "Is Justified True Belief Knowledge?" *Analysis,* 23 (1962–1963), 121–123. [Pp. 35–38 of the present volume. Ed.]

24. Harman, G. "Knowledge, Inference, and Explanation," *American Philosophical Quarterly,* 5 (1968), 164–173.

25. ————. "Lehrer on Knowledge," *The Journal of Philosophy,* 63 (1966), 241–246.

26. Harrison, J. "Does Knowing Imply Believing?" *The Philosophical Quarterly,* 15 (1963), 322–332. [Pp. 155–170 of the present volume. Ed.]

27. ————. "Knowing and Promising," *Mind,* 71 (1962), 443–457.

28. ———. "Mr. Malcolm on 'Knowledge and Belief,'" *Analysis*, 13 (1952–1953), 69–71.

29. Hartland-Swann, J. "'Being Aware Of' and 'Knowing,'" *The Philosophical Quarterly*, 7 (1957), 126–135.

30. ———. "Logical Status of 'Knowing That,'" *Analysis*, 16 (1955–1956), 111–115.

31. Heidelberger, H. "Knowledge, Certainty, and Probability," *Inquiry*, 6 (1963), 242–250.

32. ———. "On Defining Epistemic Expressions," *The Journal of Philosophy*, 60 (1963), 344–348.

33. Lehrer, K. "Knowledge, Truth and Evidence," *Analysis*, 25 (1964–1965), 168–175. [Pp. 55–66 of the present volume. Ed.]

34. ———, and Thomas Paxton, Jr. "Knowledge: Undefeated Justified True Belief," *The Journal of Philosophy*, 66 (1969), 225–237.

35. Lemmon, E. J. "If I Know, Do I Know That I Know?" in Avrum Stroll (ed.), *Epistemology*. New York: Harper & Row, 1967, pp. 54–82.

36. MacIver, A. M. "Knowledge," *Proceedings of the Aristotelian Society*, Supp. Vol. 23 (1958), 1–24.

37. Odegard, D. "On Defining 'S Knows that p,'" *The Philosophical Quarterly*, 15 (1965), 353–357.

38. Rynin, David. "Knowledge, Sensation, and Certainty," in Avrum Stroll (ed.), *Epistemology*. New York: Harper & Row, 1967, pp. 8–31.

39. Saunders, J. T. "Beliefs Which Are Grounds for Themselves," *Philosophical Studies*, 16 (1965), 88–90.

40. ———. "Does Knowledge Require Grounds?" *Philosophical Studies*, 17 (1966), 7–13.

41. ———, and N. Champawat. "Mr. Clark's Definition of 'Knowledge,'" *Analysis*, 25 (1964–1965), 8–9.

42. Sosa, E. "The Analysis of 'Knowledge That P,'" *Analysis*, 25 (1964–1965), 1–8.

43. ———. "Propositional Knowledge," *Philosophical Studies*, 20 (1969), 33–43.

44. Taylor, R. "A Note on Knowing and Belief," *Analysis*, 13 (1952–1953), 143–144.

45. Unger, P. "Experience and Factual Knowledge," *The Journal of Philosophy,* 64 (1967), 152–173.

46. Urmson, J. O. "Parenthetical Verbs," *Mind,* 61 (1952), 480–496.

47. Wang, Hao. "A Question on Knowledge of Knowledge," *Analysis,* 14 (1953–1954), 142–146.

48. White, A. "On Claiming to Know," *The Philosophical Review,* 66 (1957), 180–192.

49. Woozley, A. D. "Knowing and Not Knowing," *Proceedings of the Aristotelian Society,* 53 (1951–1952), 151–172.

Notes on Contributors

Alfred J. Ayer is a Fellow of New College and Wykeham Professor of Logic at the University of Oxford. He is the author of *Logic, Truth and Language, The Problem of Knowledge, The Foundations of Empirical Knowledge,* and most recently, *The Origins of Pragmatism.*

Roderick M. Chisholm is Professor of Philosophy at Brown University. He is the author of *Perceiving: A Philosophical Study, Theory of Knowledge,* and numerous articles in philosophical journals.

Edmund L. Gettier is a member of the Philosophy Department at the University of Massachusetts at Amherst.

Alvin I. Goldman is a member of the Philosophy Department at the University of Michigan at Ann Arbor.

Jonathan Harrison is Professor of Philosophy at the University of Nottingham and the author of several articles in philosophical journals.

Keith Lehrer is a member of the Philosophy Department at the University of Rochester, the editor of *Freedom and Determinism,* and the author of several articles in philosophical journals.

Norman Malcolm is Professor of Philosophy at Cornell University. He is the author of *Knowledge and Certainty, Dreaming, Ludwig Wittgenstein,* and numerous articles in philosophical journals.

Colin Radford is a member of the Philosophy Department at the University of Kent at Canterbury.

William W. Rozeboom is a member of the Center for Advanced Study in Theoretical Psychology at the University of Alberta.

Brian Skyrms is a member of the Philosophy Department of the University of Illinois at Chicago Circle.

Peter Unger is a member of the Philosophy Department at the University of Wisconsin at Madison.

About the Editors

Michael D. Roth received his Ph.D. from the University of Illinois and is Assistant Professor of Philosophy at Franklin and Marshall College, where he has taught since 1966.

Leon Galis is Assistant Professor of Philosophy at Franklin and Marshall College, where he has been teaching since 1965. He received his Ph.D. from the University of North Carolina at Chapel Hill.

Index